Easy Eloquence

For Kari —
You're a great speaker!
You make it look easy.

So nice to work with you —
All the best.

Susan

Praise for *Easy Eloquence*

Fantastic tips on presentation skills. I really like Susan's way of simplifying the task of putting an effective presentation together. Essential reading for all of those who present – no matter how small or large the audience!

Audrey Clegg
Director of Leadership Development, Wolseley

This is one of the best books I have read about making presentations and public speaking. Susan made the strategic importance of an excellent presentation come to life. A must to read for professionals and executives who have to make regular (public speeches and) presentations!

Rudi Plettinx
Vice President, EMEA, Center for Creative Leadership

Finally – the keys to successful public speaking in a succinct and focused presentation. Ms. Huskisson has found the Rosetta Stone to put us all at ease and enjoy the accolades!

John Scully
Managing Partner, SPO Partners

Easy Eloquence

Presentation tips for people who *hate* public speaking – but *love* the applause

Susan Huskisson

THE LONG ACRE PRESS

TUNBRIDGE WELLS ■ UNITED KINGDOM

The Long Acre Press Ltd
28 Cambridge Street
Tunbridge Wells TN2 4SJ
www.longacrepress.com

Post-it Notes

Post-it Notes are, as everyone knows, those fantastically useful repositionable bits of paper that you can write on and then stick to paper, whiteboards, your refrigerator, or whatever. I have been using them for years in my work, as you will see as you read this book. I have used the phrase "Post-it" rather than "sticky note" because that is what everyone I know calls them. Post-it is a registered trademark of 3M but for purely aesthetic reasons I have only used the ® symbol the first time I refer to them in the text and not thereafter. The use of the name does not imply any endorsement of this book by 3M.

First published in the United Kingdom in 2009.

British Library Cataloguing in Publication Data
A CIP record for this book is available from the British Library.

ISBN: 978-1–904995-53-1

Printed and bound in Great Britain by
CPI Antony Rowe, Chippenham and Eastbourne

Typeset and design by Lexden Publishing Ltd

Contents

Chapter 5: Mind Your Language!   63

Chapter 6: Visuals – a Boon or a Bane?   73

Chapter 9: Checking Out the Location   123

Chapter 10: Bad News, Tough Questions and Crises   139

Dedication

For my father – Harry Huskisson – who taught me how important honesty is in communication. And for my sister – Judy Rhyne – who taught me to balance honesty with diplomacy...

Acknowledgements

I appreciate the time and insights given to me from business leaders who shared their ideas, stories and experiences for this book. Especially:

Marshall Antonio, President, FPC of Arlington Heights

Karen Bird, Owner, Strategic Marketing Services

Beat Blaesi, Head, Leadership Development, Bank Julius Baer and Company

Philippe Brun, Site and Operations Director, ST Microelectronics

Audrey Clegg, Director of Leadership Development, Wolseley Plc

Ted Glaser, Owner, Alternate Design

Reinout Van Lennep, former Global Head of International Banking, ABN AMRO Bank

Mark Kench, Managing Director, Lexden Publishing

Anna Kotrba, HR Business Partner, ABN AMRO Bank

Mauro Maternini, Head of Zurich Branch, ABN AMRO Bank

Stephen Partridge, Managing Director, Long Acre Press

Javier Perez, President, MasterCard Europe

John Scully, Managing Director, SPO Partners

Alan Tawil-Kummerman, Chairman, Silentsoft, SA

Nathan Thomas, former ABC news correspondent

Special thanks

A special thanks to Mike Johnson, a great speech writer and collaborator for this book.

Introduction

I began this book for a good reason – because I was asked to. For years participants at my various presentation skills programmes have asked me to put everything I know into an easy-to-access format. The result of those requests is this book. My objective has been not to produce just a book of "Things to Do," but to give some flavour of the craft of creating a good presentation and describing the thrill when you not just meet but exceed an audience's expectations.

But this book is more than just the collected do's and don'ts of speechmaking that I have acquired over the years, it is also about why being an excellent presenter makes good, solid practical sense for anyone with even the slightest ambition to succeed.

There is no doubt that the ability to present well opens doors that would otherwise remain closed – especially in the professional world. Being a confident, charismatic presenter adds another talent to our list of skills and marks us down as different from others. If you are the person that your boss feels able to call on when the big occasion comes along, you are in that special category of those who are considered a safe pair of hands.

The ability to speak well, to come across clearly and confidently in public is a great talent to have and develop. It gets you noticed and it takes you to places you would otherwise never see or experience. Over the years, I have met many talented, extremely competent second-in-command executives who were overlooked for that top job simply because they were not good communicators. Believe me, being able to present effectively and convincingly is the hallmark of a well-rounded manager.

Like any other skill, being able to present effectively and consistently takes work. As I state throughout the book, it is the preparation and the rehearsal that produces that outstanding performance. Like the athlete, dancer or musician, being able to talk well in public is usually based on hours and hours of practice, but it pays off.

Here's a story that illustrates just that.

Some years ago, I was on the board of the San Francisco Chamber of Commerce. The members included some of the top corporate executives of major international corporations – Bank of America, Bechtel Engineering, Chevron Oil to mention just three – in addition to other small and medium sized Bay Area businesses. The Board held an annual retreat in Napa Valley where ten or so speakers were invited to an early breakfast meeting. We had all attended a very late dinner the night before, and many of the Board members had golf and tennis dates as soon as the meeting ended. Needless to say, we were a tough, tired, time-pressed audience. One after another the speakers approached the lectern with their notes, spoke for five minutes and left. The audience waited patiently for the last presenter, a young man from a large engineering firm. Unlike the other presenters who had gone before him, he had no notes. Not only that, he bypassed the lectern and stopped directly in front of the assembled Board members. Even before he had said a word, I noticed a few people had sat up and forward in their seats to listen – paying a lot more attention than they had been. He spoke for five minutes. He was straightforward, articulate – and confident. As he was leaving, a number of these very senior executives turned to each other and said "who was that young man?" Boy, had he got their attention!

Being in the communication business for most of my life, I shouldn't have been surprised that this young man's ability to appear at ease in front of the group would result in their immediate respect. Indeed, the experience reinforced for me the importance of being able to present well to any level of audience at any time. Having worked with many corporate presidents and CEOs over the years, I know that they too – despite their lofty status – often experience "stage fright" and anxiety when presenting. Here they saw a young executive, well prepared and confident, just the way they would like to be.

My own experiences in trying to improve the presentation skills of business professionals show that fear and the lack of time to prepare are two of the biggest barriers to my clients' feeling confident in front of an audience. And yet, in today's world (both professional and private) the ability to stand up and speak well is a skill that is universally required, and universally admired too.

I met that young man from the Chamber of Commerce meeting later and worked with him on many projects, quickly coming to respect his *substance* as well as his *style*. But in the five minutes he had in front of that Board meeting, the audience could only glimpse his capabilities by looking through the window of his style.

That young man had understood one of the key points of presenting, know what you want to achieve in the time you have. He knew that the few minutes allotted to him were possibly the only time he would get a chance to impress a group like that. He went right for it – and it worked. He gained not just respect, but recognition too.

Having worked abroad for the past twenty years, I have seen this scenario played out all over the world – from Asia to Europe to the Middle East and the US – people in charge respect those who can stand up and present well.

This book is intended to help presenters who are trying to manage their normal daily tasks while juggling the extra burden of presenting their ideas to others. Few companies give their employees a day off to go home and write these presentations, so they are developing these messages on the fly, in spare moments (few and far between) and usually at the last minute.

Many of these people are perfectionists who wait for a big block of time to work on the "perfect presentation." That large segment of available time usually never comes – and the speaker is left preparing in the small hours the night before. Through this book, I want to give you what I provide in my courses and coaching classes – a fast way to be well prepared and confident without spending an enormous amount of time that you can probably ill afford.

I have been a professional speaker, speech writer, and speech coach for more than 25 years. My audiences have ranged from a cozy cabal of just two to many thousands. I was fortunate to have excellent training when I was very young, and then the chance to sharpen those early skills into something that has allowed me to practice professionally all over the globe.

My approach is practical – not theoretical. It was, and still is, aimed squarely at busy people who, for the most part, would rather do anything *except* speak in public. As part of that process, I designed a speech model so that anyone could quickly and logically outline their thoughts. Later, realizing that PowerPoint would play a major role in presentations, I developed some visual assistance for those who need slides to make their points more effectively.

And today, being able to present applies to almost everyone. When I first began teaching others to present, most of my clients were sales and marketing people. Now, technical staff, financial executives and human resource managers are asked to speak just as often. After a coaching session, most of my clients tell me that they feel much more confident and comfortable in the role of presenter. They know what to do (and, just as importantly, what not to do) and the simple techniques to help them be more creative while developing their message in a very short time. This book is designed to help you in the same way. You can use the quick model for developing presentations in a hurry, and then try the more creative, entertaining tips for the times when you have the luxury of time to prepare.

Most of all, this is not a book of lists. It is a narrative of how to get up on your feet and feel good about the experience. Enjoy the book and the practical advice, stories and anecdotes that are a key part of it. I'm sure of one thing – it will make you a better presenter. And you will enjoy the experience more. This book is for people who *hate* public speaking, but *love* the applause. And after all, isn't that what you want?

Susan Huskisson
Marbella, Spain
February 2009

Chapter 1

All About the Basics

"Eloquence is the power to translate a truth into language perfectly intelligible to the person to whom you speak"

Ralph Waldo Emerson

"Genius is the ability to reduce the complicated to the simple."

C. W. Ceran

Getting in front of an audience – be it Boy Scout troop or the Board of Directors – and getting them to listen to you, really listen to you, is a great skill to have. But to be a good presenter you don't have to be born with that talent. Apart from one or two, most great speakers I know worked at it long and hard. The good news is, if they can do it, so can you.

If presentation success isn't based on natural talent, neither is it based on getting up and rambling on about your chosen subject for 30 minutes or an hour. Presenting opportunities come in all shapes and sizes. There is no single way to reach an audience – everyone is different and you need to craft your message to suit both yourself *and* the audience you want to reach and influence.

As I wrote in the introduction, it can be just a five minute slot. But if you use it right it can make all the difference to your career – even your life. The pop artist Andy Warhol wrote about everyone's 15 minutes of fame. For many of us that 15 minutes has been pared down to a lot less than that. We may only have five minutes, maybe just a sound-bite to get across what we want the audience to know. And in this connected up, media dominated, YouTube world we live in, it is better to be savvy and smart and understand at least some of the basics of how to reach out to an audience. Why? Because every single one of us will at some point need to "present" in one form or another. So it is a lot better to be prepared for that inevitability.

And it isn't just about speeches at sales meetings and professional conferences either. Today any responsible citizen can find themselves in the media spotlight from one moment to the next. In fact the chances are extremely high that you will be interviewed on radio or TV at some time in your career. Don't you think you'd better be ready when the moment comes around – even if it is only 15 seconds, rather than 15 minutes of fame? That 15 minutes of fame is a myth. In reality, a 15 second sound-bite can translate into 15 hours or 15 days of so-called fame (see Scenario 6 in Chapter Two).

Many opportunities just happen in everyday meetings, when you make a comment or ask a question, especially when people don't know you all that well. Think about it, the way you "present" a question or an idea says a lot about you to your listeners.

We also need to realize, that it isn't just about what we say, it's about how we say it and what we look like while we are in the spotlight. The phrase "dress for success" was never more true than when you are about to go on stage and speak in front of 2,000 people!

But the overriding issue is, what do you want to get across to the audience, what is the single thing you want them to take away from what you say? It doesn't matter if it is a one minute TV interview or an hour behind a lectern. The rule is always, always the same. What do you want the audience to think and do?

In my long experience working with thousands of would-be presenters, I see the same two basic mistakes being repeated over and over:

- No clear objective
- PowerPoint madness

Mistake Number One – No Clear Objective

Far too many would-be presenters get it wrong from the word go, because they get the reason for doing the presentation completely wrong. They begin with unbounded enthusiasm (or unbridled dread), without bothering to sit back and reflect on what they really want to get out of this. Basically, it's good to be selfish. Ask yourself the simple question, "what's in it for you or your team?"

Susan Says
You must know exactly what you want that audience to take away with them. When you rethink your objective, I bet it isn't what you first had in mind either.

Think about it this way. Your boss calls you and says, "You're going to present this year's budget plans at the next sales meeting." The first two things to ask yourself are, what do I want out of it and what information does the audience need to leave with?

So it isn't about delivering a line of figures at all. It's about satisfying the audience and putting you in the spotlight at the same time.

Anyone who has ever had to deliver a numbers-based presentation knows one thing for certain, numbers can look good, bad or downright ugly depending on how you talk people through them. Therefore, the starting point here is to go back to your boss and say, "What do you want the audience to hear?" There's a lot of room to do a lot of very different things with a basic brief like "present next year's budget."

Look at it this way, just by how you stack up the numbers you can:

- make the budget look aggressive and innovative
- make it look safe and attainable
- make it look challenging, but reward-driven
- show that your team needs additional resources to do a better job

By making sure you have the right emphasis on the right places you can make your audience:

- be deeply concerned for their future employment
- feel good about the products and services they are selling
- highly motivated to go out and meet the challenge of making next year's sales target

We know which you would choose, but is your presentation geared to options one, two or three? All too often, I see managers delivering presentations that are guaranteed to turn off even the most enthusiastic employee. It doesn't have to happen if you know – from the outset – what you want the audience to go away with. I don't mean lie to people or be untruthful. Indeed, always tell the truth. But shape your presentation to meet the needs and the expectations of the audience. Usually, deep down inside, the audience wants you to succeed and you want the same for them.

The same goes if you're asked to present at an industry conference. What do you want the audience to hear? Do you:

- want to tell them about your product, service or idea?
- want them to rush out and buy your product, service or idea?
- want to have people investing in your product, service or idea?

Three very different objectives. But which one do you want to get across; what do you want that audience to do when the presentation is over?

Or could it even be that you:

- want to scare the competition with your superior product, service or idea?
- want your competitor's best people to switch to your business?
- want the competition to hire you at a much bigger salary?

Three more possible objectives. But which is the one for this audience, at this time, at this conference?

Mistake Number Two – PowerPoint Madness

I have one very big rule that I stress at the beginning of every class I teach: "for now, *leave the PowerPoint alone*!" Under no circumstances turn it on. You don't need it just yet. Maybe, just maybe, you won't need it at all (more about that later in the book). Let your objective and your structure drive the PowerPoint visuals – not the other way around.

Sock 'em With Your SOCO!

What I've been leading up to here, in getting you to think about the *real* objective of your presentation is to underscore the importance of having it right from the beginning. No matter how pressed you are for time, taking a few minutes to think through the logic of your presentation and what it is supposed to achieve pays off hugely at the end of the day.

Knowing what you want to achieve and then working out how to say it are what I call the *Single Overriding Communication Objective* (SOCO). Believe me, no SOCO means no result.

Sure you may have some other things you'd like to get across, but every presentation ever made has *one big thing* that it needs to achieve. I don't care what it is, all I care about is that it works – every time. For example you could have three key objectives to get across, but that's not your SOCO. Consider this. Your objectives are:

- explain your product's key advantages and benefits
- emphasize your product's reliability record
- publicize the dealer network

Your SOCO is to get the audience eager to rush out and buy it!

Having said that, in other cases your SOCO could be to have members of the audience ask you to come and demonstrate it; or sign up for a franchise or a dealership.

As you can hopefully see by now, if you don't know what your SOCO is you can't begin to develop a presentation, for the simple reason that you don't know what outcome you want. As the saying goes, "If you don't know where you're going, any road will do." That's not what professional presenting is all about.

Over the years that I have been teaching people how to prepare a presentation I've seen a great deal of vague and unfocused thinking surrounding the reasons for giving a presentation. And even if it is the same presentation – one you know really well and feel good at delivering – every audience is different. So in every case, revisit your reasons for doing it and what the real SOCO is this time. You'll be glad you did.

To help you, think about those three objectives I listed earlier. You want to:

- tell them about your product, service or idea
- persuade them to rush out and buy your product, service or idea
- have people investing in your product, service or idea

These can be, essentially, covered by the same presentation, the only thing that changes are the parts that emphasize the "inform", "buy" or "invest" parts of the story. But if you don't have the audience clearly in mind and what it will take to get them to remember and hopefully do what you want, then the whole exercise is a waste of time.

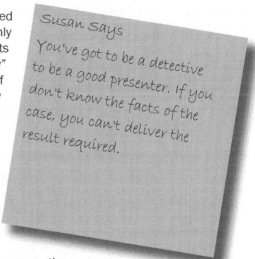

Susan Says

You've got to be a detective to be a good presenter. If you don't know the facts of the case, you can't deliver the result required.

And a waste of time is exactly how you can describe many presentations from people who should know a whole lot better.

Many speeches are unfocused, because the presenter couldn't be bothered to do the homework. Others are the victims of sloppy preparation or plain arrogance. The "I'll just give that stuff I used last year" approach. That simply isn't good enough. You need to know key things before you step onto that stage:

- what is the overall context of this presentation – other speakers, conference theme and so on?

- who are the audience? – by which I mean what do you know about their culture, background, level of knowledge, attitudes, and any issues that might affect them?

- for international audiences, what is their level of understanding of the language you will speak?

- how many of them are there?

- what are their expectations?

- what do they know already?

- how long can I speak?

- are there any limitations: physical, technical?

- what's my objective with this audience?

Once you have answered all of those, you can begin to think about the basics of your presentation. The raw material, the bare bones. Always lay out the bones first, you can add the flesh and even some blood later!

The backbone of the presentation

The backbone of your presentation is your SOCO. That is what anchors everything else. So my advice is, sit back, relax and think about what you want to get through to this audience. Just what is that single overriding communication objective? To help you further in developing that SOCO, think of it this way:

- do you want to get the business?
- get another meeting?
- just introduce yourself and your organization?

What your priority is defines how you structure the presentation. Remember, we'll get into all these areas, item by item further into the book.

Ask questions

You must ask questions. You need to ask whoever requested you to give the presentation about the audience. Make sure that the person who is giving you the information really knows and understands the participants. Some sources are a whole lot more reliable than others. Talk to some of the audience members for suggestions when you can.

The next step is to ask yourself what you feel most confident telling the audience. Identify information that you feel the most secure in presenting.

You need to ask yourself (and tell yourself the truth please!) what is the best way to get across what you want to achieve with *this* specific audience. Don't forget every audience is different, and until the day you can walk out onto a stage and "feel" what the audience needs (and there are very few people who can ever do this), do your research and be ready.

Armed with that knowledge you can begin to put together a presentation that is relevant (to the needs of the audience and to you too), achievable and meets the time constraints set for it.

I like to outline the presentation and leave the structure for awhile. Once the structure is in my mind from that simple exercise, I discover many useful items to put into the presentation. A news story or event, an anecdote, a good example will become more meaningful when I am inadvertently looking for material for the presentation. This is called 'subliminal problem solving.' My mind is constantly searching, even unconsciously, for information for the next speech.

Reinout van Lennep, former Global Head of International Banking for ABN AMRO Bank and an outstanding speaker, describes this way of developing material as having your full concentration (unbeknown to you) focused on that next presentation. Too many speakers wait until the last minute to prepare (mostly perfectionists who keep waiting for a big block of time that never appears) and miss so many opportunities for creating great material.

Keep things simple

You want to keep things as simple as possible. Don't try and complicate the process or the message. If this is your first time in the big time, keep it *very* simple. You don't need fancy material. You just need to reach the audience with a direct message that they can understand easily. That way you'll be certain to deliver a successful message and that will build your confidence for the next time. I am a great believer in building confidence over a series of successful presentations. Just like climbing a mountain, you learn a little more every time and you move a little higher up in your abilities.

Keep things short

Please, please, please keep things as short as you can decently get away with. No audience likes someone who goes on and on, who bores the pants off people. Keeping it short is at its best when people actually wanted more of you. Learn that short is sweet, very sweet indeed.

Also don't make the mistake of trying to cram too much into that time slot you've been given. Give yourself elbow room in there. Time it, work at it, cut it back as you need to. Just don't lose the SOCO in the process.

That focus on keeping things short can extend beyond presentations. Javier Perez, President of MasterCard Europe and another fine professional speaker, makes everyone stand at some of his meetings for the duration. He reckons it cuts down on meeting time and keeps people 'moving' to accept new ideas. He says "Long speeches are a sign of weakness." Most senior executives I know feel exactly the same. The shorter the better.

Pace it nicely

Trying to say too much in too short a time means that you can't pace yourself. Speakers that are the most appreciated by audiences know how to organize their presentation time and in doing so they come across as confident and competent. Pacing yourself means that you know how long your presentation takes and you can keep it nice and steady all the way through. There's nothing more likely to turn an audience off than a speaker who suddenly realizes he has only a few minutes left and tries to get every last word in. Here's a rule to present by: Think Simple, Think Short, Think Pace.

Susan Says

Once you've written your presentation, try and leave it alone for 24 or 48 hours. I bet you'll make at least one significant change when you come back to it.

Also think tick-tock. Yes – a clock! I have the habit of always carrying a very small clock with me and I place it on the table or lectern when I begin. I find watches too clumsy or difficult to read. Just make sure you have disabled the alarm.

Use positive speech

Using negatives creates just that, a negative atmosphere. Be positive, upbeat, proactive. Use action words, verbs and adjectives that rouse the audience and grab their interest. I don't mean oversell, just give it some pizzazz and make the audience as excited about your message as you are. Make sure you end with solutions – not problems.

Rehearse, rehearse, rehearse

Finally, please, please, please make time for rehearsals. Going over and over your presentation really does make it better. You can do this on your own initially, but, wherever possible get a colleague to help you. And listen to their suggestions and criticisms. Remember they are the audience. What may sound great to you may not come out that way.

One last thing to remember when you rehearse. Typically – in fact almost always – you'll find that the real-life speech takes you around 25 percent longer to deliver than your rehearsal. Make sure you factor that in.

Ready, Steady, Take AIMS!

Now, let's look at how to put a presentation together. Follow the guide below and you should be able to put together a basic presentation inside an hour. No, it won't have every bell and whistle on it, but it won't have any material that shouldn't be there either and it will get the message across.

I've been developing this model over many years. The reason I think it's ideal is because you can use it anywhere, in almost any circumstances. It's called the AIMS! model, and it is built around five things:

● **A**cceptance: an opening that gets the speaker accepted by the group he/she is addressing
● **I**nterest: an introduction that secures interest in your speech
● **M**essage: the body of the presentation (80-90 percent of the speech)
● **S**ummary: underscores those key messages and provides the next step (for the audience)
● **!**: yes, that's an exclamation mark. Stands for making a closing impact!

Now I'll let you into how I got to this simple, yet effective way to develop a winning presentation.

Writing down what was natural to me

I had been making speeches for many years when someone asked me how I wrote my presentations. I realized that I had – unknowingly – developed over time a simple, easy system for creating practical presentations. I was like a chef with a popular dish, but I had no recipe for it. So I sat down one day and thought through what was "just coming naturally" to me. The AIMS! Model is the result of that analysis.

First, as I pointed out earlier, I find out as much as I can about the event and the audience. In later chapters I will elaborate the questions you should ask here, but just remember *one size does not fit all!* And, as I have stressed, at this stage, don't turn on your computer. Don't open PowerPoint. Just find out about your audience and the basic requirements of the presentation, that's all you need to do.

Then, identify the *objective* for your presentation and remember that it is going to change each time you present. If you don't bother to change it, then don't expect the reaction you would like to get from the audience.

While seeking out your objective, consider this. There's an architectural term "form follows function," and that is also true for presentations. Determine your objective (the function) and the form of the presentation (the words and pictures) will be much easier to construct.

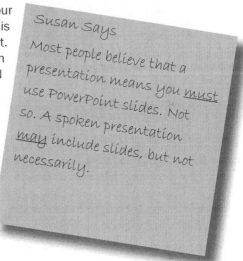

Susan Says

Most people believe that a presentation means you <u>must</u> use PowerPoint slides. Not so. A spoken presentation <u>may</u> include slides, but not necessarily.

Setting objectives

Any speech has to have a clear objective. Exactly what do you want the audience to do or to know by the end of the presentation? And like any objective it must be both measurable and achievable.

Simply hoping that senior management will think your proposal is a good idea is not measurable until you determine what they will *do* if they think it is a good idea. Going on from there, is it achievable given the audience's knowledge of the subject, the resources available or the time in which you have to deliver the material?

Don't forget that you can have both short- and long-term objectives for presentations. In the first presentation, your measurable, achievable objective might be that the group invites you back for more intense discussion, or that you can do a feasibility study. For the second, return presentation, you may hope that the audience writes you a cheque! But if you ask for the money in the first meeting, your objective, while measurable, might not be achievable.

Moreover, if your objective is to provide information, be specific in identifying what information you want them to have. Usually, you cannot really teach in a speech, only inform or create a spark of interest. So limit the amount of information to be consistent with the level of knowledge of the audience and the time you have to speak.

Think of it like this. You couldn't teach a group how to play golf in ten minutes, could you? But you might be able to demonstrate how to hold a golf club. And that is about all you can hope to do in the time available. As I have said before, one of the biggest mistakes I see speakers make is trying to do too much in the time they are given. In presentations there are only ever two options, either negotiate more time or limit the material.

Usually you hope that the audience will *use* the information you give them, so your objective is not just passing the information to them, but encouraging them to use it (do something with it) in a very specific way. Therefore, poorly thought out or vague objectives just don't work. You need concrete objectives that audiences can relate to and act as hooks to hold the presentation up.

My advice, based on a lot of experience, is to try and visualize your audience doing something different because of your presentation – and that action (what you want them to do) becomes your objective.

So set your objective before you begin to write the actual presentation.

Now try to outline your material using these layers for what you want to say – always keeping your objective in mind.

Acceptance – the opening

Start by gaining acceptance from the audience. Let them feel comfortable with you as the speaker. Usually look for something you have in common with them – common background, interests, problems, values, experience, reason for the meeting, the conference theme, even the last time you met with them. Basically, anything that provides a link and a hook to get them to feel good about you. I find that once I identify common ground with my audience, I feel more relaxed as well. One of the reasons this common ground is so important to acceptance by the audience is that so few speakers bother to find it. This kind of opening lets the listeners know that you know who they are and that you took the time to find that common link. It creates a comfort zone that makes both you and the audience feel good inside. It also creates an emotional link between you and the listeners.

Interest – the introduction

Here you want to gain the audience's interest in what you will tell them. Create a need for them to listen to you. Assume that the people in the room are also busy and you need to remind them that what you say is important to them. Tell them what you are going to tell them. Identify your topics, but be sure to tell them the WIFM (What's In It For Me). Create a value added promise as you give them the roadmap of your presentation.

Message – the body

This part – which is meat in the middle, is about 80% to 90% of your presentation. It is like the present you give someone, and the rest of the speech is the gift wrapping. Divide your message into no more than three major topics, each backed up with Examples and Evidence that reinforce your message and are tailored for that specific audience.

Summary – tying all the pieces together

Remind them of the parts of the presentation you most want them to remember and then tell them what they should do next (your recommendation, next steps). This is the time to take any questions from your audience to make sure that your message has sunk in.

!!!!! – closing with impact

After you take the final questions, have the last word with the audience. Motivate them to do what you want them to do. Remind them of something you said in the beginning, tell them a story or a quotation that underscores what you have been saying. Challenge them or simply close with the headline – the most important point you want them to take away.

Never close with phrases like, "thank you for your attention" or "thank you for listening." You do not want to leave them with an apology for taking their time. End with solutions – not problems. Remember – be positive and proactive.

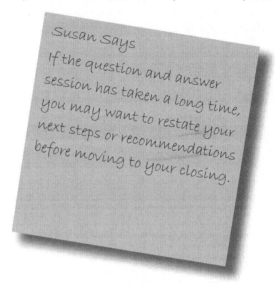

Susan Says
If the question and answer session has taken a long time, you may want to restate your next steps or recommendations before moving to your closing.

Using the AIMS! Model to Build Your Presentation

Now that you understand the basic flow of the AIMS! model, you can build your presentation. Start by taking a Post-it Note ® and writing down your SOCO. This doesn't form part of your actual presentation but it should guide every single element of it so you need to have it up front and visible the whole time you're working on it.

Now set aside Post-its for every element of your presentation following the AIMS! model. Bear in mind that you will need six notes for the body of your presentation – one for each of your three main topics and one each for the corresponding supporting examples. Allowing an additional Post-it for questions gives you a total of 12.

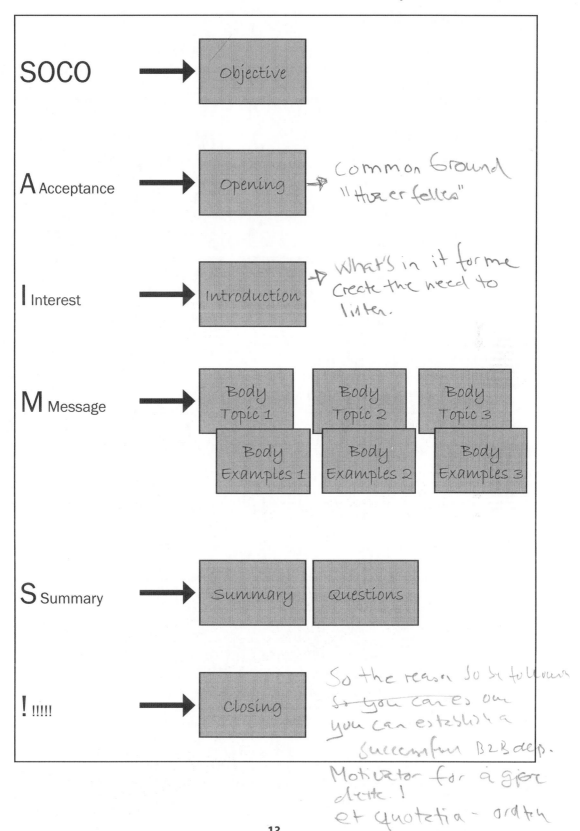

SOCO → Objective

A Acceptance → Opening ⟶ Common Ground "Hueer felles"

I Interest → Introduction ⟶ What's in it for me Create the need to listen.

M Message → Body Topic 1 / Body Topic 2 / Body Topic 3
Body Examples 1 / Body Examples 2 / Body Examples 3

S Summary → Summary / Questions

! !!!!! → Closing

So the reason So be following
so you cares our
you can establish a
successful B2B dep.
Motivator for a goal
delte. !
et quotetia - ordth

To make it easier to see where you are, and how your presentation fits together you can use the template in the Appendix at the end of this book. For a larger version (A3), you can download it from the website www.speechworksintl.com using the password: AIMS. Here's how the downloadable AIMS! storyboard will look:

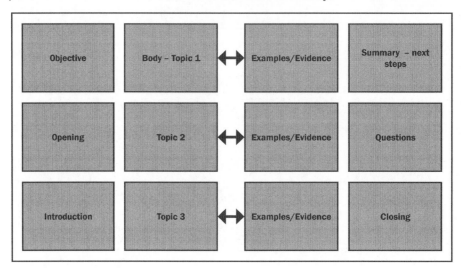

One of the best parts of the AIMS! model is that you can give the same presentation many times, (roadshows) and just change the opening and examples to fit the audience. You don't have to write a whole new presentation.

Take your Post-it Notes ® and put them on the appropriate squares, writing in (as briefly and succinctly as possible) what you want to say in each part of the model. This system uses square Post-it Notes (approx. 7.5cm x 7.5cm – 3x3 inches). Small Post-it Notes force the user to keep the notes as brief and to the point as possible. This first outline lets you construct the message framework first, then fill in the details later.

Susan Says

Both the template in the book and the template on the website have been designed to use standard size Post-it ® Notes. This means that you can write and rewrite, edit and correct your presentation as many times as you want. The other great thing about this is that it is a totally portable system. You can use it anytime, anywhere. You don't even need electricity!

Start with your objective. You can fill in anything as the idea comes to you. Once you have your objective, you can move down vertically to the opening – what I've called "your common ground with the audience" – or you can skip to another square.

Indeed, it doesn't matter in what order you complete the notes, since it will all come together like a crossword puzzle. Just make sure you set your objective first, then go in any order you like. The Post-its make it easy to reorder and discard material as many times as you wish.

When you finish you can look at the AIMS! grid and see how everything fits together. Finding examples and evidence that back up your topics and persuade and inform your particular audience is important. Also it is useful to spend time looking for examples that you believe will most relate to and convince the audience you have to address.

If you set good objectives from the start and spend some time filling out the grid, you can have an excellent presentation inside 60 minutes. Not only that, but you can use the grid over and over again – creating a core message but being able to add openings and closings and examples and evidence that meet specific audience needs.

From that point – when you have more time – you can start making the basic model something more exceptional. Do this by developing great openings and closings, identifying persuasive and more entertaining examples and evidence.

But the AIMS! model really comes into its own when time is limited it gives you focus and discipline to hit the key must have points quickly and painlessly. It also gives you the "helicopter view" of your message, so you can see how everything fits together (or what doesn't fit at all), and how it reinforces your objective at the top. What's great about doing it this way is all you need are a couple of pieces of paper and some Post-it Notes to make it work anywhere. No lap-tops, no PowerPoint required (at this stage). You can work on the plane, train, in your hotel room. Anywhere in fact when the idea strikes you. Just take the AIMS! folder, a package of Post-its, and go!

Here's what the story board layout will look like. You fill in the details on each post it.

Each square is a part of your presentation – it is *not* a slide. Add the appropriate slides after you draft the presentation structure – not before.

Start with your SOCO, the Objective of the presentation (don't write any more until you identify your purpose) then move to the Opening, Introduction, Body (3 topics) Summary, get ready for questions, and finally the Closing. Once you identify your objective, you can fill the post its in any order. I usually write the opening last because it seems to be the hardest part.

Chapter 2

Exploring the Presentation Universe

"Every time you have to speak, you are auditioning for leadership."

James Humes, author and
former US Presidential speechwriter

So far we've looked at some of the basics of the presentation process with the objective of getting you into the right frame of mind to stand up in front of an audience. Then I've taken you (at the end of Chapter One) through the AIMS! Model – a really quick-start method for getting a workable presentation together. Now what we need to look at is the cold, hard reality of the presentation game. In fact, much of what this book is about is getting you to put presentations as a familiar system into the everyday context of your work. I strongly believe that the presentation process shouldn't be about something extra, but be just another part of the skills – the professional skills – you need to have. It is just one of the ways you deal with the responsibilities of your job. And as we all know, no job is ever perfect for long. Be honest, we never get to do all the things we like all the time do we? So it is with presentations. What I want to do here is give you a frank, been-there-said-that introduction into the wonderful world of presenting.

For instance, most times when you pick up a business or management book you enter a parallel universe. A world that seems devoid of office politics; jealous, devious or conniving work colleagues and bosses with real human failings. But we all know that these clean, tidy little worlds – invented by business school professors to fit neatly into their theories of organizational dynamics – don't match up to day-to-day reality. Similarly in the real world presentations aren't made by comic-book style heroes, as in the – hero stands in for boss – hero gets standing ovation – hero gets promoted – scenario.

Not at all. In the real world, presentations usually begin something like this:

Scenario One: It's Friday afternoon, you're cleaning up your desk for the weekend. You have plans. Then your boss puts her head around the door. "I'm so glad I caught you," she says, "I have to go to an urgent meeting at headquarters next week, so you'll have to stand in for me on that presentation we've been preparing." In a nanosecond your plans for the weekend lie in pieces. You nod, unable to say anything. Words form in your head: *me, presentation, next week.*

Scenario Two: You're sitting over lunch with your best client. They're really pleased with you and the service you're giving them. So impressed that the managing director says, "We'd like you to come to our annual top management meeting and present your ideas." That fine glass of wine turns sour in your mouth: *best client, top management meeting, my ideas.*

Scenario Three: You're at a conference; you've sat through a day of dull, lifeless, uninspiring presentations. Over a drink in the evening you rashly blurt out your thoughts on what the presenters *should* be saying. "Great," says a voice behind you, "thanks for volunteering!" It's the senior vice president of manufacturing, a man who could – and would – make or break your career. "I'll put you on as the closing speaker at our next event," he says . You're thinking *me, closing speaker, next event.*

Scenario Four: Congratulations! You've got a new job. Everyone's delighted. So much so that your new boss slaps you on the back and says, "Jacques, great to have you with us. Now I want everyone to get to know you as quickly as possible, so what I've planned is to get you to give a short presentation to the employees on Friday. Nothing too elaborate. Just share your vision for our future will you?" Your euphoria vanishes as quickly as it came: *all employees, vision, future.* You have your own, very private vision of what your future holds if you mess this up!

Scenario Five: Your company holds its annual international conferences in exotic locations throughout the world. It's an honour to be invited as one of the speakers – great visibility and an exciting trip. You have always wanted to be one of the selected speakers and this year, your time has come. Someone has cancelled and you are one of the conference presenters and workshop leaders: *me, in front of senior management and a thousand people.* Careful what you wish for!

Scenario Six: The company is in crisis. Mass layoffs and a plunging share price. The communications director is tearing out his hair. Finally he gets to you. "Amy," he says, "I need to get a consistent story out there to make sure that the employees and the outside world get the same message all the time. "Great idea," you say, "couldn't agree more." Then he says, "You're the one that has to do it, there's no one else." Five minutes later you are outside the gates of the factory facing six TV cameras and 30 microphones. Yes, you just may be in that very position sooner than you think.

These six scenarios are real. They've all happened and I can guarantee that one or two of them are happening to someone, somewhere, right this minute. Like the rest of our working life, presentations – getting on your feet in front of other people – are rarely planned. They come at us out of left field and slap us on the chin when our guard is down.

Sure there are occasions when you are in control 100 per cent of the way, but mostly, in that real world that we have to survive and exist in, being asked, told or just plain ordered to present is not a planned exercise at all. And this leads me to something else: most advice on giving presentations that I've heard seems to start with the question "why do you want to do it?" The true answer to that in the majority of cases is because it's what you have to do. There's no choice, no "maybe" about it.

But it's at this time that the professional in you needs to come to the surface. It's fine to ask to present when you are really organized and have honed a speech until it gleams. It is quite another thing altogether to be told to present – often at short notice – with no ifs, buts or other excuses allowed. And let's be honest here, that's usually how it begins. But it doesn't have to end that way. Not if you're smart about it, at least.

Here we come to one of the very first rules of presenting anything. You must always do it in the very best way you can, no matter how it started. Anyone who doesn't "get" this from the outset – no matter how onerous the task may appear to be – is going to let themselves, their organization and their colleagues down. OK, so you don't want to do it. But you haven't got the choice have you? So, let's not moan about it, let's give them the best darn speech they've ever heard!

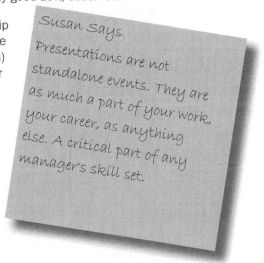

Susan Says

Every speech counts. Every speech must be the _very best_ speech you can give. There's _never_, ever an excuse for making a sloppy speech. There's an old Tennessee saying that fits making presentations to a tee – "Do a little, but do it well."

This is the point where we truly separate the real professional presenter from the rank amateur. Because it isn't just about presentation. It's about your whole attitude to work and career. One of the biggest mistakes people make is thinking of a presentation – any presentation – as a standalone event. It isn't. Never was, never will be.

Get Good At It

Making a presentation, whether to your team, your work colleagues, a customer or any group whatsoever is just a part of doing business. Why? Because it is more or less inconceivable that anyone in business today – no matter what business – can avoid having to stand up in front of others and explain, exhort or extol their views and ideas. Presentations are a major part of our working lives. So, it stands to reason that we might as well get really good at it, doesn't it?

Audrey Clegg, is Director of Leadership Development for Wolseley, a large (revenues more than £16 billion) British company. As part of her responsibilities, she looks for new talent for this very successful company. Audrey, an excellent and accomplished public speaker, describes the importance of being able to speak well by saying, "everyone must sell themselves and their ideas in today's environment – from the job interview to the board proposal."

Susan Says

Presentations are not standalone events. They are as much a part of your work, your career, as anything else. A critical part of any manager's skill set.

More than that even. I believe that the ability to make effective presentations, wherever and whatever the circumstances are a key part of the skill set of any effective manager in today's business environment. Don't have that ability and you are missing out on something important.

So, now we have defined – and hopefully agreed – one of the key elements of presentations – they aren't an "extra" in the routine of business, they are a part of everyday work-life, part of "doing business as usual."

As a matter of fact, maybe the word presentation isn't always the right one. I'm reminded of some words of advice a colleague was given many years ago on his first day at a new company. One of his mentors wisely explained that for the first days and weeks he was – as the new person on the team – very much a curiosity. "Don't forget," he counselled, "in those early days even asking a question is a presentation. You are on show."

Susan Says
Presentations are not just formal events. Every time you ask a question in a meeting or volunteer an opinion, you are "presenting." You may be sitting in the line of vision of your organization's top management when they are making a presentation, and that senior group is left with an impression of you before you ever say a word.

That's advice he's never forgotten. Too many business professionals don't think that way. However, it's good to remember that a "presentation" doesn't have to be formal or planned. You are effectively presenting every time the spotlight focuses on you.

What we need to do now is begin to look in more detail at what presentations involve. How do we construct them; what help can we get, what are the building blocks you need to use? Using the AIMS! model as the primary building bloc we are ready to expand the concept to help you design many different types of presentations.

The first thing to get right is what kind of presentation is it? While that might seem like a simple question to answer – it isn't.

Reason? There are as many different types of presentations as there are days in the year. But getting it right from the outset is the key and knowing what type of presentation you need to make solves many of the initial problems in getting started.

Presentations come in – literally – all shapes and sizes. Simple and short to small groups – complex and lengthy to big groups. Explanatory, motivational, confrontational, informative, persuasive, entertaining. Keynotes, ceremonial, facing hostile audiences. Technical, top management, sales conferences, training and development. Each and every one of these breaks down into multiple categories and permutations, and we haven't even addressed presentations to groups outside your immediate circle – stakeholders, pressure groups, politicians and public servants. Neither does this cover additional complications like audiences in other countries, with language limitations or different experiences and aspirations.

As I said, the list is endless. But the good news is that there is one common denominator in all this – *you*.

You and your desire and drive to give the best presentation you can, whatever the circumstances. To understand and accept that presentation skills are just as much a part of today's workplace as any other aspect of your skills and responsibilities. Your promise to yourself to meet whatever presentation challenge in the most professional way possible.

Be a Detective!

To be an effective presenter – one that gets it right every time – we need a touch of Sherlock Holmes in us. While we don't have much use for the deerstalker hat, cape and pipe, we do need the legendary detective's powers of observation and his ability to ask and get answers to awkward questions.

Because what we are going to do is hunt for clues. Clues that can help us solve what remains a mystery to others – how to create and deliver a great presentation that meets the needs of the audience and – more important – you too.

In true detective style we are going to set out and answer the following: Who? Why? What? Where? and When?

Why we are doing this is that one of the biggest failings of presenters anywhere is their complete lack of understanding of what the presentation is about, the context it is being given in, the audience's expectations and the real, desired outcome. Indeed, most presentations fail for a simple reason – arrogance and a "can't be bothered attitude." Too many of us think we have all the answers. How often have you heard colleagues, say "oh, I'll just change a few things in that speech I made last year – that'll keep them happy." No, it won't. Being unprepared, being sloppy, fixing up some old presentation says a great deal. It says (in red neon lights) that you don't care about the audience and it says a great deal about you too. So this "why" goes beyond your SOCO to why you, personally, want to do the most professional job possible.

Who?

There is always someone who is a trigger for a speech. A work colleague needing help, your boss, your boss' boss, a customer – the list is endless. But it is vital to think through how it was that you were asked instead of someone else. It is vital to know what is expected of you. If you don't have those pieces of information, how can you deliver?

Inside the business

Who asked you? If the request has come from inside your business it probably isn't too hard to work out what you have to do. If your boss asks you, then there are several possible reasons. The three most likely are:

- they are too busy to do it themselves
- they want to give you an opportunity to use this as a learning experience
- they believe you are the best person to deliver this message

Either way it doesn't matter, they are all opportunities to show what you can do. Whatever anyone else might think this is the paramount goal for you. This is your opportunity – take it.

Outside the business

If the request has come from outside then you need to consider carefully why they asked you and what was their reason for doing it? This can have all sorts of implications when you bother to think about it.

- it is an opportunity to showcase your business, but more importantly *you*.
- it is an opportunity to get in front of a group that can help you and your firm in the future

The audience (the other "who")

From there you need to consider who is the audience? We will go into more detail on this in Chapter Three, but this is a vitally important part of any preparation. This is the first time we really mention the audience, but it is a key thread running right through this book. The audience is the most important part of all this – never forget that.

Look at it this way, if you don't know who the audience will be, you can't possibly deliver a presentation that meets expectations, never mind going beyond them. Not knowing the audience is possibly the biggest mistake that any would-be presenter can commit. It is about as sensible and as dangerous as trying to drive your car down a six-lane highway in rush hour with a blindfold.

Get to know the audience in as much detail as you can. Not just who they are but what they think you will tell them, what they believe in and what they expect to hear. From that you can build your presentation, meet *their* needs and get *your* message across. Never underestimate the importance of recognizing the values of your audience.

Who else is speaking?

Another critical piece of information that is so often overlooked is knowing who else will be there. Of course, if you are the sole presenter that makes life easier, but it doesn't mean that you are really on your own. For example, if it's a presentation to a client or customer will you be alone or will there be others from your company? Will the boss be there, possibly someone even more senior? Never forget that opportunities like this work on many different levels. OK, so you wowed the customer, but did you wow the boss at the same time? Remember, it isn't just about the audience, it's about everyone who will be there – including from your side.

Likewise, knowing if you have others speaking before or after you helps you position what you say and how you say it. If there is a really strong presenter, try and get on first or last, never just before or just after. Picking your time can be crucial, and even great presenters know that sharing the spotlight can be just too much.

I prefer being the first speaker, if possible. The first presenter tends to set the pace of the program. Also, most people tend to go over their time slot, which means later speakers wind up cutting material because the show is running late. Once, in Singapore, I was the last speaker for a conference where the presenters before me took more than an hour longer than expected. Luckily, I had anticipated this possibility and came prepared with two presentations – the original one and the short one – Plan B!

I know there are some professional presenters who will argue that if you are on first your message gets forgotten, but I don't agree. The advantages of being able to give your delivery while you (and your audience) are fresh, with your time slot intact, means you come across as professional and highly organized.

Getting on early in a program also means that you have the rest of the time to meet informally with the audience. Go on before lunch and all you see are the backs of hungry conference-goers as you wind up your session. Go on at the end of the day and everyone's heading out for that train or plane.

Being the first speaker at a conference makes you the Keynote speaker (good publicity) and sets the tone for the entire conference. Be sure to tie your start to the conference theme and use short quotable comments so that the following speakers refer to your comments for the rest of the session.

Another key "must", is to make sure you link to other presenters. Picking up on what others have said, or what they will say helps the audience fit all the pieces together. It also makes you appear very knowledgeable and professional. I was surprised when speaking to a Rotary Club once that I followed someone who talked about ostrich farming. It was a stretch to try to link my presentation to that topic! I learned to ask about other speakers and then to ask *again* right before the event.

Why?

Of course, it certainly helps to ask why you were invited to speak, particularly to get to know the real reason for your sudden popularity, but more important than that is to ask yourself that question: "why am I doing this?" Seems to me a very legitimate question to pose yourself well before you start thinking of wise and witty phrases to startle your audience with.

Many presenters flattered by an invitation never ask themselves the question "why?"

Many a hapless employee never bothers to ask "why?" in the face of a direct order from their boss.

Few managers told to prepare a ten-minute presentation for the top management meeting bother to ask themselves "why?"

This seems a great shame to me. It means their presentation is being built around a reactive response to a command rather than creating a proactive opportunity. The difference between reactive response and proactive opportunity is only as far as your imagination and enthusiasm can take you.

What I am suggesting is this: why be reactive and produce, at best, a mundane, run-of-the-mill presentation when for the sake of a few hours of hard work you can make a memorable, lasting impact?

Susan says

Asking yourself "why?" you are making a presentation should deliver the answer, "because it is an opportunity for me and/or my team".

Remember, this book is about *you*. Getting you to believe in yourself and getting you to bypass the easy option and use presentations as a key part of your way of doing business. Presentations are not one-off events; they are an integral part of today's business. So, to ask yourself "why?" is critical. It is to remind yourself that in making a presentation (no matter how it first came about) you focus on what you want to achieve. Of course you must meet your SOCO (single overriding communication objective) but at the same time you can also make the speech work for you at a personal level.

Realizing that the "why?" is about creating an opportunity, is part of getting you into the right frame of mind to deliver presentations that always meet everyone's objectives – the audience's, the organizer's, your organization's and your own.

What?

Just what sort of presentation have you been asked to make? As we saw earlier there are hundreds of permutations, so it is very important to get this straight from the outset. Obviously a five-minute slot on a crowded meeting agenda is very different from an hour in front of a large audience. But is it? My view is that we need to regard every opportunity as just that – a chance to show your abilities. This isn't about showing off, it's about making others realize that you (your team, your group, those other charity volunteers) are a safe bet for whatever comes up and also someone who feels comfortable talking about their business, its people, products and services. And don't forget, every audience, no matter how small, affords an opportunity – often an opportunity that isn't visible at first sight.

Again it is that ability to be a good detective that comes in handy. Find out just what is in store for you. Who are the organizers; how long do they want you to talk; where will it take place; what's the audience and what is the theme? Knowing all these things helps you build up a picture in your head that meets the organizers' needs and your own.

Remember the SOCO from the earlier chapter – the Single Overriding Communication Objective? Well, many of us never get this completely right – leading to disappointment for us and others. That's why it is so important to know as much as possible and make sure that it is *your* Single Overriding Communication Objective that gets met – not theirs. You don't tell them that, of course. In fact you give them what they want while ensuring you get what you want. Think about it this way: organizers might want you to talk about how you achieved the amazing product penetration you did. You on the other hand want to show that the product or service is great and that you are the power behind it. Or it could be that you are asked to demonstrate some cutting-edge technology – fine for the organizers. On the other hand, your SOCO is to convince the audience that you and your team should be hired to develop this technology in their business.

Subtle differences in approach and emphasis, but critical to how you develop the material and deliver the end result.

Get it? Got it? Good!

Where?

Knowing the location of the presentation is also important, so important that I have devoted a large part of Chapter Nine to it. But a few things are key. Having some basic facts about where you are going to present can be very useful, even control and dictate the type of presentation you create. So make sure that you quiz the organizers to get as much information as possible about the physical space you are going to be working in. Don't forget that you are doing this to help *you*. Whatever happens you don't want to turn up at a venue and be surprised by the set up. All too often a failure to check out facilities can result in turning what should have been a great presentation into a poor one – even a disaster. Not only that, setbacks do one thing – destroy your confidence. And a rule to keep in mind: the further you get away from your own location the bigger the problem gets (just wait until you get to Moscow, Mumbai or Manila and find out that Murphy's Law[1] really does exist!). So find out all you can about where you will be speaking – you won't ever regret it.

When?

If the presentation the boss has dumped on you is tomorrow morning at nine there's not much point in trying for the Churchillian delivery, the show to die for where timing is everything. However, there is every point in making sure you keep it simple, simple, simple. Don't try sophistication, don't try complexity (no fancy IT or visuals either), just keep it as straightforward as you can. One thing you can do though is grab someone and test it out on him or her as quickly as you can. Guaranteed if you're on the platform tomorrow, you'll have forgotten one thing or failed to include something vital. And always, always, always get someone to hear you rehearse your opening and closing minutes. What are you going to leave the audience with? Very few presenters – even the best – are clever enough to leave it to chance.

Susan Says

If it's a last minute invitation to speak keep it very simple. Use the AIMS! model in its simplest form. Don't take chances, make it short, but very sweet!

If, however, you've got a week or a month to prepare, then you can begin to work on it and make it work for you. How much time you have is critical. If you've got a month, use it, don't wait until the last minute and then panic. Use the time to rehearse and get to know more about the audience and the venue. If you've got time don't squander it, use it wisely and it will repay in the end result.

One other word of warning. If you ever get asked to deliver someone else's presentation, make sure that the audience knows that from the outset. Don't try and be smart and pass it off as though it's your own. State quite clearly that you were asked to stand in at the last minute ("Mr Smith regrets he cannot be here today, but he's asked me to give his presentation") and deliver the message. While you may want to be associated with the message, you may not want to have the audience criticizing your delivery because you gave someone else's material at the last minute.

---

1   Murphy's law is an adage in Western culture that broadly states that anything that Can go wrong WILL go wrong – at the worst possible time.

Every time is important

Every speech is important for one, simple reason – you never know who is listening to it. An old colleague of mine was asked to present as part of a series of Winter Talks at his local community centre. Being a busy person, he was somewhat reluctant to do it, but after suitable pressure was put on him he agreed. One dark winter's night he went along to present, and faced an audience of just nine locals. Undeterred he gave it his best shot. His presentation was informative, lively, humorous and met with wild enthusiasm from the tiny group. But there was more than just appreciation. One member of the audience was so enamoured by his skills on the platform, he asked him to feature on a local TV show. He has never looked back, except to be thankful for the time he said "yes" not "no" to his local community's request.

The Six "B" Words

Throughout my career I've had a belief in six simple words that have become my touchstone. Every time I think I am getting above myself with my ideas, too complex, too wordy, I go back to them. So should you.

Here they are:

- be prepared
- be logical
- be simple
- be positive
- be yourself
- be professional

What I am emphasizing in all this Who, Why, What, Where, When is that you need to treat presentations the same way as any other part of your job. They are not extra. They are not something you prepare for when everything else is done – they are an intrinsic part of your everyday job. While there may be some of your work colleagues who may never, ever master the art of talking to an audience, that doesn't concern you. Being able to explain and train, amuse and defuse, excite and unite adds not only new skills, but valuable ones too. Skills that are usually quickly recognized. Being confident and comfortable in a presenter's role adds to your list of talents. Who do you think your firm will ask to present at a critical time? Not the most smooth or glitzy, but the man or woman who can do the best that meets the needs and strikes the right chord time after time after time. It's called being professional. And that's what you are going to be.

Chapter 3

Setting the Stage for Great Presentations

"The fool tells me his reasons; the wise man persuades me with my own."

Aristotle

"Fools rush in where angels fear to tread."

Alexander Pope

First thing we must all remember – it is the audience that defines the scope of the presentation. If you don't know who you are talking to and why you are talking to them, you may well be sunk before you start.

While the message may be important (and it is), if you don't know the needs and expectations of those you are going to present to you may as well spend the day in bed. Audiences govern what you say and how you say it. All too often, I have seen would be presenters reach for their notepad, lap-top or whatever and start sketching out a presentation. Only thing they have forgotten about is who they are going to speak to and why.

Many of us – busy, stressed, piled up with work – think it is all too easy to put that speech together or use the one that worked last week. I can tell you that without knowing who your audience is it won't be successful. OK, you may get away with it once or even twice, but sooner or later the audience will find you out.

Smart presenters, professional presenters all have one thing in common – they respect the audience. It doesn't matter how big, how small, the audience rules. Don't forget that – ever. What I want to show you in this chapter are two very separate things: the external presentation and the one we often forget about (but is equally important) – the internal presentation.

The External Presentation

You're sitting in your office, the phone rings. It's your pal Jim, Director of your local chamber of commerce on the line. "Can you come and talk to some of our members next month," he says, "give us some of your experiences in marketing?" You're delighted. "Of course, you say, count me in."

OK, that should seem a safe bet, shouldn't it? A friendly call to make a presentation. No problem, no sweat, you are all too happy to oblige. Not only that, but your boss thinks it's a great opportunity too. But stop here and think. Aren't there some questions you should be asking yourself? More importantly, aren't there some questions you should be asking your friend Jim at the chamber of commerce?

Consider carefully now, just what have you said "yes" to? The invitation looks perfectly above board. All you have to do is create your presentation and show up and deliver it. That's right isn't it?

No, that's *wrong*.

Susan Says
Connecting with the audience begins a long time before you ever meet them. Do your homework on who they are. If the people who invited you are slow to give you this information, keep pushing for it. This presentation is your performance - not theirs.

Why is it wrong? Because you have just volunteered to walk into a minefield without a mine detector. It's worse than that. You have actually volunteered – willingly, even enthusiastically – to stand up in front of a group of people you have never met and tell them about yourself, your product, your business. You have no idea who these people are, what they think of your products, why they are in the audience. Moreover, you have no idea what their mood will be, what they are expecting from you or, for that matter, what opportunities might exist?

What you need to do now, long before you think about creating that presentation is find out about the audience. Because if you are going to "wow" them, you need to know as much about them as you can? You need to be a detective again.

So get back on the phone and call Jim. And the kinds of things you need to ask him are:

- what is the size of the audience?
- what information will the audience had already received about me before the event?
- do you know the types of people who will be there and their level of experience?
- can I get a list of names, job titles and companies before the event?

Why do you need to ask these questions? Well I'll tell you. All good speakers turn up at the venue – wherever it is – armed with as much knowledge about the audience and the event as they can get. Reason? If they are properly prepared they can meet the audience's expectations and achieve their own. Result? Everyone's happy.

What I am now going to do is take you item by item through the list above and explain while all of this advance intelligence is important.

These questions to ask are in no order of importance. But it is a useful checklist to keep with you every time you find yourself having to make a presentation.

Gosh! They're all women!

A senior researcher I know produced a study about women in business. It was an instant hit and got lots of publicity. As a result, he was invited to Amsterdam to talk to what he thought was a group of Dutch managers. Well it was. Only problem was he didn't read Dutch – and therefore didn't understand the invitation brochure they sent him – so he arrived to give his presentation to be greeted by 400 women executives!

He told me later that he now understood what women presenters had been going through for years (talking to largely all male audiences) and he still had nightmares years later of looking down on a sea of female faces! (I must observe here that as a woman, I would have never been surprised to see an all male audience!). Remember, remember, remember, ask, ask, ask!

What is the size of the audience?

There is absolutely no way that anyone can meet the needs of an audience unless you know how many of them there are going to be. I don't mean down to the last person, but presentations take on a completely different tone depending on whether there are six, 16, 60 or 600. Obviously if it is a small group it tends to be a lot more informal and there is a lot more eye contact and opportunities to interact. With larger groups (over 100) you lose the coziness and the informality. Indeed, large groups can be very, very daunting the first few times you have to speak to them (more about that in Chapter Seven). So your first order of business is to know how many people you are going to be addressing. Sounds like a sensible thing to do, right? You'd be surprised how many people turn up at a venue and then ask: "How big is the audience today?"

How long should the presentation be?

You must know how long you have to talk before you can begin to plan the presentation. For example, you can't say much in five minutes, but you can say too much – and really bore people – if you go on too long. Also be ready to challenge the amount of time you have been given by the organizers. If they have only given you 20 minutes and you know you need 30 to fully explain what you are trying to get over to the audience, say so. Conversely, if they ask you to do 90 minutes and you know you can't fill that amount of time, tell them. The one thing that both presenters and organizers don't like is surprise. When you get onto that platform and you know you have to speak for 20 minutes and you are fully prepared for that. Remember, don't be bullied into agreeing to something that is going to be impossible to deliver on. OK, try it once and you'll very quickly see what I mean.

What type of room will it be?

Again, over the years, I have be amazed by just how many people show up to make a presentation with no idea what the room they are going to "work" in looks like. Personally, I can't see how anyone can deliver a great presentation if they don't know anything about the space where they will be working. The room and the venue are so important that I cannot stress enough that you must get the organizers to tell you as much as they know (often not as much as they should). I'm not suggesting you get paranoid about it, but really think through what you are going to present and how the room will affect you. Today, thanks to the Internet, we can normally get pictures or floor plans of most venues. I usually send in advance a complete list of equipment and materials I will need, as well as a layout of the placement of all of the equipment. To say it again, make sure you make that call and get as much information as possible, including the type of equipment they have to make sure it is compatible with your needs. The physical space and the equipment you will need are so important that I cover them in more detail in Chapter Nine.

> **Susan Says**
> Have the screen for your slides on the side and you stand in the more central position. You are the message; slides should back you up – not dominate the room.

Is a question and answer period expected?

You get onto the platform, you give your presentation, what happens then? Do they clap and then sudden silence; does someone say, "Mr X will be happy to answer questions"; does anybody actually ask a question? Even great presentations can end very, very badly just because no one bothered to think through what happens when it's over. If you want to take questions the time to say so is when you start. And it is you who need to tell the audience that. Say, "I'll be looking forward to answering your questions and hearing your opinions at the end." Even if you are introduced (see later), make sure that it is you who are in control, and you who ask the audience.

Equally, if you want to take questions during the presentation (personally I hesitate to do this unless it is very informal or there is plenty of time because it can derail the presentation) say so from the outset. However, my experience is that if you have a carefully prepared presentation, stopping and starting it tends to make it very uneven (you can even lose the thread of your argument) and is likely to make you run over time.

Then again, if you don't want questions, say that too. The worse thing is to be left standing there

> **Susan Says**
> Don't be shy about planting questions in the audience. It's about making you look good, otherwise why be there? And the planted question(s) can help kick-start the rest of the audience into posing their own questions.

in front of an audience in an embarrassed silence broken only by the chairperson finally saying, "Well let me ask the first question." That's an awful way to end a presentation you have put your heart and soul into, isn't it? Of course, remember that your closing always follows the final questions, no matter how many you have.

If you think this can happen to you, there are two things to do. One, be ready to move off the platform as soon as you have finished your closing. Remember, they can always bring you back again (which, by the way, looks good). Second, get some questions planted in the audience before you begin. While this might not seem the most honest way of getting audience participation, it more often than not sparks off genuine questions from the audience. All you need to do is make sure that the organizers identify two or three people who can do this. It does make your presentation look a lot more valued and they are more likely to remember it. The other way to stimulate questions from an audience is to be deliberately controversial or move them out of their comfort zone. However, that presumes that you are comfortable with – or even enjoy – questions from an audience that might not completely agree with your point of view.

Susan Says
Remember to move to your closing following the Q&A part; don't let the audience close for you, leave them with the message YOU want them to have.

I often present to audiences who have English as their second language and are shy to speak in another tongue (even with interpreters). I break the audience into smaller groups that identify questions (they are not so shy with fewer people) and then receive questions from the individual groups. Having the audience submit written inquiries or comments is another (not very dynamic – but effective) way to solicit participation.

Don't forget that a lively question and answer session can add a great deal to your presentation. The trick is getting it going at the start. Most audiences, especially where most of them don't know each other, are always reluctant to ask questions. Once one or two people have get started, that breaks the ice and it becomes easier for everyone. And while I advise using a little humour (but be careful, it can backfire on you), I can't end without mentioning the way former US Secretary of State, Henry Kissinger used to initiate responses at press conferences, by saying, "What questions do you have to my answers?!"

Who will introduce me and what information do they need about me?

Being a professional presenter means being in control of all aspects of your presentation. This includes what others say about you. So don't be shy – *ask*. You need to find out not only who is introducing you, but what they intend to say about you. If you don't you risk one or more of the following:

- Being introduced as someone else (oh yes! It happens!) or having the wrong job title or speech topic

- Being introduced as an expert on something you've never heard of (that happens too!)

- Being introduced by someone reading out your biography, which doesn't really have any relevance to what you are about to speak about. That long biography has the audience bored with you before you've had a chance to say anything

That means that as part of your preparations you need to send the organizers a short note with the details you want emphasized when you are introduced to the audience. What the chairperson says colours how the audience sees you when you first get to the platform. As with everything else, make it clear who you are. Don't have them disappointed before you start. You can even give them the script of what you want them to say about you if you think they'll agree to that.

Finally, if for some reason the chairperson doesn't follow your suggested introduction do it yourself. Clearly state: "Thank you for that introduction. I would like to add ....." Don't forget, your, presentation, your introduction, your audience. It is you who are in control. For the 30 minutes or whatever you are on that platform, it is your event, no one else's. Then again, don't be tempted to over-correct the person introducing you. No need to make an enemy of the chairperson!

Susan Says

Keep in mind that your body language during your introduction is very much part of the first impression for the audience. If you are reading your notes during that time, you may look bored with your own introduction. Look mostly at the person introducing you, visually reacting to the comments, and occasionally looking at the audience.

Years ago, I attended a speech by former Colorado Senator Gary Hart to students at a University in Paris. Hart had run an unsuccessful campaign for the US presidency. Part of his political failure arose from the media reporting some supposed "extracurricular activity", to put it delicately! The student who introduced Hart spent an unbelievable amount of time describing *not* Hart's distinguished career, but the media reports of his escapades. Hart had to sit on stage throughout the entire introduction that described in minute detail his exploits. To Hart's credit, when he began his presentation, he said, quite briefly, "I believe your introduction will be longer than my speech....and, really, you shouldn't believe everything you read in the Washington Post." Hart's brief acknowledgement of the embarrassing intro, that bit of humour, and then rapid movement into what he had to say was an excellent way to regain control. Still, it would have been a good idea to have known what the student planned to say before the event.

Are there other speakers?

Of course you need to know if you are the sole attraction or you are sharing the platform with others. If there are other speakers what you need to do is think carefully through where you would ideally like to be on the program. The reason for doing this is to make sure that you get the most out of the audience. I suggest you go first in case someone else plans to cover parts of your topic. Clearly, early coordination with the panel will help avoid this problem. Once again, keep in mind why you are doing this – to reach an audience with your message. That's it!

Relating to other speakers

Other speakers on a program create all sorts of opportunities. Number one, is that you can always learn from other speakers and most of them are only too pleased to talk. I find that watching other people's presentation techniques helps me think about my own – either what I can borrow or what I can be sure to leave out!

Then again, there are the great, natural presenters who seem to make speech after speech with little or no effort. Most times that "no effort" style has come after a great deal of hard work. Few, if you can get them to admit it, ever found it easy at the start. Mind you, there's one thing you might want to avoid with the really good speakers, getting a slot that is too close to theirs. Being on before a well known speaker may consign your session to the trashcan of memory for most of an audience (who often only came to see the "star"). Being on after is often just that – an after thought. Having said that, I have seen "back up speakers" (like some back up bands for famous music performers) who "stole the show" by doing such a great job. You could be one of those. If you feel you are following a really good speaker, then just do the best job you can to be your most professional self. Your own style could well be a nice contrast to someone else's.

Susan says: Remember that a professional speaker always "listens and links" to other speakers on the same program - even those who might be coming later in the day. That's also a way to hook up to the star speaker.

Tapio Hedman, a Senior Vice President at Nokia, had the (mis)fortune to follow Al Gore (who had just won a Nobel Peace Prize) on a forum. Tapio worried about presenting after this famous speaker, so he worked hard to create a substantive and entertaining presentation. The message was crafted with stories, music, and power slides. His endeavours paid off and his session was hugely successful.

Suffice it to say that any smart presenter – no matter how much of a rookie – probably needs to get as far away as possible from the black hole that surrounds any major speaker. Distance yourself, you'll be glad you did. Having said that, don't forget to go and hear them. Guaranteed you'll pick up some ideas.

Will there be a panel discussion?

To my mind, most panel discussions are poorly planned and, therefore, usually achieve pretty poor results. Often this is because they are invented at the last minute or used to fill up some time. The worst thing that happens is that the chairperson invites the morning's four speakers to join him or her and then asks the audience for questions – as if these will materialize like magic. Sadly, it rarely works out that way.

The other horror is that all the questions go to just one person – normally the most interesting – leaving the others sitting there like ducks in a shooting gallery. The expressions on their faces and overall body language, sadly say it all.

Susan Says

Watch out for your body language when you are on a panel. Even if you are not answering a question, the audience can see you. Look interested, not bored, please.

For successful panel discussions, as with everything else in this business, preparation is 99 percent of the process. First things first, do you want to be on the panel at all? Ask yourself, will it do me any good, will it give me the kind of exposure I want to the people I have come to meet with – the audience? If you are going to sit there like a dummy, while the star of the event gets all the questions, avoid the panel at all costs. If you are going to sit there while the audience gets bored to death – avoid it. But if you do agree, then, as with your presentation, prepare, prepare, prepare!

Here's what you do:

Make a short, specific statement that comments on the presentations of the morning or whatever. Simply say, "Mr Chairman (or whoever), before you ask for questions, I'd like to make a quick point...." This gets you into the limelight before the others and shows you have been thinking about this session.

Plant a question in the audience to be directed to you. Don't be shy about this. You want the panel session to work don't you? Hey, your actions might just save it from being really boring.

Comment on what another panellist has said by saying: "Let me add a point to what John has just said..." Again this gets you into the limelight and shows that you are taking charge.

Remember, you are there to meet with and talk to the audience. That means that the panel discussion isn't there for self-aggrandizement, it is yet another part of the SOCO process. It is part of your presentation. If you have something to say, *speak up*! I often see panels where one or two people never say anything. Later, they admit they would have liked to add something, but were too shy. Do make thoughtful comments during these sessions, even if you have to force yourself. It's worth it. (The same is true for the everyday meetings you attend).

Push the conference organizers to have participants sign up for the panels in advance. This knowledge will help you plan what to say and what to be ready for.

Am I expected to turn up for my session or attend the whole event?

Unless you are super-pressed for time, my view is get to the event as early as you can. That way you can sit in the audience and size them up. Get a feeling of their mood, how they react to other speakers, really get to know some of them by talking at coffee breaks or whatever. Also, if you are confident enough, try putting a few points made by others speakers into your own presentation. That helps the audience connect with your ideas and puts it all into context. Take the opportunity to talk with other speakers and especially the chairperson (remember that introduction they are going to give you?), to get their feelings about how it is going.

Susan Says:
Don't just rely on those assessment sheet results that organizers give you after the event - they don't always tell the full story. They are often based on a tiny sample of the total audience and not necessarily representative.

I also like to "meet and greet" people in the audience before my presentations. That way I feel I "know" them before I start.

The same after your presentation slot. Sit in the audience and see how they feel, try and get feedback on your own session. Often it's better to get quick, off-the-cuff, honest reactions right away than hear it from the organizers later.

What information will the audience have already received about me before the event?

Presenting – particularly at outside events – usually means that there is a website link, brochure, program or catalogue prepared to be sent to participants before the event. All too often we send in our CV or resume and leave it at that. Now why would you do that? Again, think. This is the first opportunity to reach the audience. What you want is for them to know who you are, what you do and what you stand for before they see you on the platform. So take some time to get that pre-event message loud and clear. Make sure that it reflects what you are going to talk about and what you want to communicate to them – that SOCO again.

If they require a picture please, please, please don't use the spare ones from your passport application! Get some really good photographs taken (professionally) and have them easily available. Best way is to have them on a website so that organizers can download them as they require them.

The same goes for the material that organizers might want to put into a seminar or conference notebook. Make sure it meets the SOCO that you have set. All of this should come together with one clear message about you and what you are going to talk about.

Do you know the types of people who will be there and their level of experience?

This can often be the hardest to pin down and every one of us gets this one wrong from time to time. The reason is that all too often the organizers themselves don't know who will be in the audience. Even a look at titles and companies doesn't always help as people send substitutes or organizers believe they have the crème de la crème when they only have the rest of the pint of milk.

However, it is important to try and get a "feel" for the level of knowledge and the role these people play in their professional lives. If you don't have some inkling of that it is very difficult to pitch your presentation at the right level. Too simple and you look lightweight. Too highbrow and you'll lose them. My best tip for this is to talk to others speakers who have been on previous events. That way you can usually get a good read-out of who will be there (often more honest and accurate that than of the organizers) and what their knowledge level is. It's also a good idea to find out if there have been any last minute arrivals.

Knowing who is in that audience can be a career maker or breaker.

Susan Says

Don't accept every invitation you get. Flattery is fine and egos need massaging but ask yourself, "Will this do me any good, will it help my career, my sales target, my reputation?" Or more simply, "Am I the right person to do this?"

We can all recount nightmares (see box) where we were badly briefed on an audience. It has happened to everyone and will continue to do so. But you do need to have some idea. The biggest problems are those big, catch-all industry events where the experience and seniority levels in the audience are all over the place. Trying to pitch to an audience like that is very difficult. All you can really get away with is the most superficial of presentations. Asked to present on one of those and you really need to ask yourself, "Should I do it?"

"They're All in IT

Here's an example of just what can go wrong unless you really, really insist and then insist some more.

A colleague of mine was invited to speak at an industry event. He went through the usual checklist, where, when, topic – everything. When he asked, "Who are the audience?" he was told: "They're all in IT. They are all senior IT executives involved with IT, and what they want is to get a broader picture of the business world today, especially current trends in recruiting and retaining talented individuals."

Seemed straightforward. What these people wanted – it appeared – was to have a general presentation on trends in business today. The idea was to make these IT people more aware of the world outside their immediate expertise.

My colleague prepared. Turned up, met the organizers. Everything was OK. Only it wasn't. Yes, they were IT people, but they weren't just any IT people. They all worked for the public sector (no one had mentioned that) and more than half of them worked for the military.

His presentation was centred on the imperative of being able to recruit top talent quickly and using creative incentives to retain them. He knew he was in trouble when one (uniformed) participant interrupted him to say: "It takes us nine months just to get the selection panel organized." From there it went downhill all the way. Moral of the story: You can never ask enough questions about your audience.

Can I get a list of names, job titles and companies before the event?

If you can persuade the meeting's organizers to give you access to names and numbers do it. This is the holy grail and means that you can follow up with an audience after the event is over. However, this type of personal data is like gold dust and you'll often find that organizers are extremely reluctant to let you have that kind of open access.

If this sort of information isn't available, one solution is to offer to give the audience more information if they let you have their business cards after the presentation is over. The other is to give them information with your website and email address on it. That works too! The handout is better than putting your contact details on a slide.

Can I bring a colleagues/staff members with me?

What's this got to do with the audience? A lot. Think about it. There's only one of you and there are possibly hundreds in the audience you are going to address. While not everyone will be interested in what you have to say, if you have picked the right venue then most of them will be. So how do you reach out to them? Simple. Get some of your work colleagues to be in the room and talk to people and give out material or samples if that's appropriate (see below). Also colleagues can provide really useful feedback on how you did, how you connected (or didn't) with the audience. It can also provide a new experience for work colleagues and be a useful learning process.

When you are trying to sell ideas or products, see if you can get a stand or a place to distribute samples and staff that with your colleagues. Use it as a real opportunity to get some of your work colleagues recognized by the audience. It also helps to have members of your team on hand who can answer questions that are outside your area of expertise.

Can I bring leave-behind documentation and how will this be distributed?

This is another important issue to get clear from the beginning. What can you reasonably bring with you to give away to the audience? Organizers of some external conferences are very specific about what you can and cannot distribute (they see your presence as something you should be grateful for!). Therefore ask right from the outset, even before you commit.

My view – especially if you are not being paid a fee to be there – is that you should insist on at least a minimum amount of your documentation to be distributed. If that isn't allowed then consider your position. Is it really worth making the effort?

Also, if you do get the organizer's permission, how is it going to be given to the delegates? Will it be on their seats when they get into the meeting room; on a table inside or outside; handed out as they leave? To make sure you get the best out of your efforts on the platform and also give the audience all the information you want to get across, it is important to make sure this is clearly agreed (in writing is a good idea).

Susan Says

When possible, I prefer "take-aways" as handouts. Any material you distribute before or during your presentation ends up competing with you for attention as the audience "reads ahead" rather than listens to you.

What are the opportunities for follow-up contact with the audience?

As we have mentioned time and time again throughout this chapter, this is your audience. But where or when does it stop being your audience? My view is that this is up to you. And much of that depends on the flexibility of the organizers.

If you are speaking at an event inside the EU then data protection laws mean that it is unlikely that you will be able to get the names, titles, addresses and emails of every person in the audience. But if you can get the details of those who have "opted in" to receiving communications then you might consider sending them a follow up thank-you note. Just bear in mind that even if they "opted in" to communications connected with the event, they probably haven't made an active commitment to communicating with you.

A better option is to seek to extend your "hold" on your audience by getting them involved in a follow-up action: a survey, a piece of research, a consumer or user panel. All these sort of initiatives extend the shelf-life of that audience you spoke to so many days or weeks ago. And they have the advantage of gaining a level of active commitment from your audience – they have chosen to take part so should be more receptive when you get in touch.

The other action you can take – especially if you have got rave reviews for your presentation – is to offer to stage it in their organization. Often this will be greatly appreciated and obviously acts as a real Trojan Horse moment. Getting into a target's own backyard so to speak.

The Internal Presentation

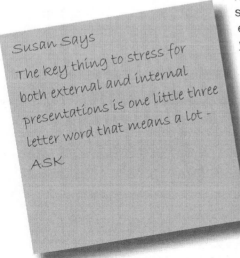

Susan Says

The key thing to stress for both external and internal presentations is one little three letter word that means a lot –

ASK

Then, of course, there's the internal presentation – sometimes known as the invitation from hell! Your email pings and there's a message from HQ "Would you like you to present a progress report on Product X to the next regional marketing meeting?" Again you're delighted. Recognition beckons at last. You turn to your laptop and start making preliminary notes.

Call me paranoid, but if it were me I wouldn't be that calm, or excited. My first thoughts would be, "Why did they ask me and what do they really expect?"

Yes, it's time to get back on the phone and ask some serious questions.

And here are some of the things you need to know:

- who will be there (in the audience)?
- who else will be speaking?
- who will be chairing the meeting?
- who are the decision makers?
- how much time have I got?
- what sort of visuals/props are expected?
- what should I bring with me?
- can I bring colleagues along as back up?
- what happens after the presentation?

And, because we all live in the *real* world, there are some other questions you need answers to before you climb onto that platform.

- are there any issues that you need to know about?
- are there any company problems that you should be aware of?
- are there any political lines being drawn up?
- are part of the audience likely to be jet-lagged?
- are these people going to be verbally aggressive?
- are there any toes I might be stepping on?
- what are the worst possible questions I might be asked?

All, or any of these can quickly doom your presentation. Watching the visiting, jet-lagged group from the East Coast nod off on the front row can demoralize the most confident speaker.

While some of these have been dealt with in some detail in the external presentation section above, internal presentations do present their own sets of issues, problems and opportunities. And while I don't want to stray into the messy world of office politics, I should say that all too often people asked to make presentations inside their organization don't take it seriously enough. As I have said throughout this book, even if the presentation is to six people, get it right or leave it alone. You never, ever know who will be around that day and might just drop in to see how you deliver your ideas! Senior VPs are notorious for turning up where they are not supposed to be.

Susan Says

I work with top management constantly who tell me they appreciate the speakers who get to the point fast, provide details only when asked, and supply good evidence for their material.

As before it's all about asking the right questions and making sure you get the right answers.

Who will be there (in the audience)?

I don't care how small the audience is going to be you really do need to know who is going to be there. There's no such thing as a "no sweat" presentation. Even if you know everyone in the room, there's always the outside chance that some visiting fireman from HQ shows up that day and says, "I'd just like to catch Mike's session, see what he's up to." Careers have been made or badly mauled on last minute decisions like this.

If it's a bigger session altogether, then again make sure you get it all right. This could be your opportunity to get in front of people you may only ever see just this once (or possibly just once a year). And I do mean getting in front of them, as the senior people usually like to sit in the front row!

> *Susan Says*
>
> *No matter how nervous you are and how much you may want to break the tension - no jokes! Funny asides about the company, hard work and so on, don't go down well, even it they are appearing to laugh! Humour, on the other hand, a funny comment or anecdote that truly adds value to the message, can break up a boring presentation. Just make sure the humour is not dangerous and that it has some value and relevance to your topic.*

Who else will be speaking?

Who's on the list and where do you figure in the line-up? Remember what we said earlier, try and pick your spot. You may beg to go first and get it over with – don't. Get a slot that means you'll get all the attention on you and your story. If your audience is tired (jet lag, late company dinner the night before) try to go first and put lots of energy into your presentation. Use some interaction (asking questions, etc,) if possible.

Who will be chairing the meeting?

> *Susan Says*
>
> *I suggest you send a short outline of your presentation to key audience people (the chairperson, for instance) to ensure your topics are in line with the meeting's agenda. And of course, make sure you have that agenda in advance.*

Who chairs the meeting can be vital for your own success. If it's your boss you've little to worry about (unless you have seriously messed up recently) and you can expect a good slot and a good introduction. He or she will probably give you some leeway on time too. However, if it's a rival or someone you don't know things might be different. If you don't know them, meet them before and find out about them. Ask if they will introduce you in a way that gives you credibility to the audience. Be prepared to give them some background if necessary. If it's a rival don't fret too much (chances are they will be as nervous as you that it all goes off well). Easiest thing to do is make it easy for them. Stay professional. Give them some notes on what you are going to say (that helps both sides) and stay friendly throughout (you can be angry afterwards if necessary!)

How much time do I have?

Timing is critical. Remember you are trying to make a good impression so start and finish on time. Use your slot wisely. Simple approaches are best. A story with a beginning, middle and end never hurt in these situations. If it is a series of presentations and timing is critical make sure you know if your time slot includes a period for questions. Why? You want questions, it makes you look good (as long as you know how to answer them). You can usually count on senior management to ask questions – *lots* of questions. They even make lots of comments as well. You might want to factor interruptions into your time allocation when you are planning.

What sort of visuals/props are expected?

If you work for an organization there's every chance they will have visual and graphic rules that are pretty much standard and you'll have access to templates that you are expected to adhere to slavishly. Personally, unless you have to make a highly complex, technical expose, I would keep it as simple and straightforward in the graphic department as possible.

Also, as I've said earlier we are all open to the "death by PowerPoint" syndrome and the last place we want to bore the pants off the audience is in front of the CEO. My thought is that if you can get really comfortable with it, you should try and do as much as you can with as few visuals as possible. Then when you do use a visual it really counts and says or stresses something important. Whatever you do, try, try, try to use as few slides as you can.

Susan Says
Particularly for senior management, avoid detail in presentation slides. Separate __data__ from __information__. Management normally wants information - not data.

This theory can easily be torpedoed depending on the kind of presentation expected and what your role is. For example, if you are asked to do a light hearted review of the year, then throw everything you've got at it. You want to be remembered, make sure they do remember *you*!

Another thing to watch out for are decrees from on high (yes, the boss) that try and set out rules on numbers of slides. I know of companies that have set limits of no more than three or four slides per presentation. This is silly. All it means is that eager beavers in sales and marketing cram 20 slides onto three, so no one can read them. Limits on the number of visuals are based on what you have to tell, not some random wish of a CEO, who's mind should be on more important things.

What should I bring with me?

As with any audience you are trying to get their attention and influence them in one way or another. So, like external participants anything you can share with them adds value to the presentation. Leave-behind documentation, emailed slides etc, all help to colour in the picture and make sure they get the message.

Can I bring colleagues along as back up?

This will probably depend very much on the session and how "closed" it is to outsiders. However, if you are able to bring colleagues or your team with you, this acts as a strong motivator. It also allows others to see the kind of people you've been able to build around you. It also gives you some back up for questions that may be out of your area of expertise.

What happens after the presentation?

We talked about post-presentation initiatives earlier and the same thing applies in an in-company scenario. Where possible try and find ways to follow-up with people you presented to. Easiest way to do that is get asked to deliver progress reports or respond to questions that have been raised in the session.

No matter what you get asked to present and by whom, never forget one thing, you need to have your personal SOCO met. Your top management may want to discuss progress on a project, next year's budget, new market strategies. That's fine, you can deliver on that. But what's your Single Overriding Communication Objective? It isn't any of those is it? Yours is perhaps to get recognition for your work; garner plaudits (or even resources) for your team; or get a promotion or a move to a more challenging business opportunity. You don't have to tell anyone else, you just need to be quite certain what it is and aim straight for it.

Best and Worst Speaking Slots

Consider carefully the best slots to take up on any program and be prepared to ask for them. Of course, you won't always succeed, but it pays to try.

First session of the day

I like to go first. The audience tends to have a higher attention span early in the program. If you know the audience will not be settled at that time (some cultures are notorious for arriving quite late) then the first slot does not work well. I have also noticed that senior management is "fresher" for this "first of the day" presentation and tends to ask more questions. That could be good or bad news depending on how confident you feel.

Last session before lunch

Anticipation is in the air and it's not aimed at you! There are whispered conversations, thumbs busy texting. Where to meet? Who to meet? Not much attention is spared for the speaker on the platform. Also at the end everyone rushes to get to the lunch room, so you'll struggle to get any people stopping by to chat. I have taken this slot and reminded the audience that they would be enjoying lunch following my presentation. This reminder helps them focus on me because they know a break is coming soon. For sure, don't go overtime with this slot.

First session after lunch

Apart from the ones who fall asleep, there are those who have stayed in the bar, gone out for a smoke, or gone to meet old friends/customers/prospects (tick one or all). Then there are the people coming back in late as well, distracting others. If your aim is to get the audience's full attention, don't come on after lunch.

Last session of the day

This is either good news or bad news and depends very much on the event and the timing. While it can be a great opportunity to leave the audience recalling your sound words of advice, that's fine if they are all in their seats hanging on your every word. More likely (and the bigger the audience the more likely it is), they are looking at their watches, gathering up their things and trying to creep out to catch their train or plane. I've seen even great speakers lose over half their audience during a closing session just because people had pressing travel plans. Everyone rushes for the exits, leaving you the lonely figure on the stage. But if you do have this slot, just as in speaking before lunch, remind them that this is the grand finale. Be sure to link to all the presentations (briefly) to show how everything in the program has led to what you are going to say.

The middle of the morning or afternoon

If you get into the middle of the program, morning or afternoon, do something to wake up the audience. People tend to pay more attention in the beginning and the end, and the middle of any session is where we have to jump start an audience.

Although keynote sessions are wonderful for the ego and visibility (hopefully!), if it is a big conference it may well be better to go for a workshop or smaller seminar session, where you can really connect with the audience. This depends on what you are selling or telling, but often has a much better response from those people you are really there for. Yes, that's right – the audience! Getting and keeping their attention is the goal.

Building a Bond Between You and the Audience

Great presenters do something that those who never take the trouble to develop and learn never can --they build a bond between the audience and themselves. They talk to the audience, not at them. They make the audience feel at ease, to enjoy the experience. They create an emotional connection with the audience.

All the really great presenters I have seen, heard and worked with have several things in common:

- they never, ever take the audience for granted, they build a bond and find a common ground.

- they never insult their intelligence by not being prepared

- they always invite their involvement as a group and – by inference – as individuals. It seems as though the presenter is talking just to you

Susan Says

For your audience, never overestimate its knowledge, but never underestimate its intelligence.

Where possible they do this by using easy-to-recognize references that are familiar to that audience (eg a complaint about the traffic they all had to get through; a reference to one of their products or their company slogan).

They pick out people and speak directly to them. In more intimate situations you can use this in greater depth by referring to people in the audience by name.

Audiences are fickle things

Then again, audiences are fickle things. They get moody and sulky, happy and hostile – even worse their boredom threshold is easy to reach. Your job is to strike a balance that makes them want to listen and leaves them wanting to know more.

If you can do that, you'll have succeeded where many have failed. The way to do it is know as much as you can about the audience long before you ever meet them. Ask, ask, ask and then ask some more.

Chapter 4

Author! Author! Openings, Closings and Great Bits In-between

"Where shall I begin your majesty?" she asked. "Begin at the beginning," the King said, "and go on till you come to the end, then stop."

Lewis Carroll, Alice in Wonderland

In my business, as you can imagine, I am constantly asked, "What makes a great presentation?" After years of listening to thousands of speeches, I am convinced that there are many ways to prepare for and give a presentation. What I bring to the party are some tried and tested techniques that will ensure success: the building blocks, if you like, of the presentation business.

It's a little like asking: "How long is a piece of string?" There are so many answers. Think of it this way, a great presentation is similar to a mathematical equation – it has constants and variables. I can give you the constants that you must have in the presentation, then you can add the variables that will make your own message something special.

Having said that, there are two things that I strongly believe underpin all the best presentations, no matter what they are about or where they are given:

There's no doubt in my mind that a good presentation is five percent inspiration and 95 percent perspiration. You get out of it what you put in. More of that later

Every good, great or totally unforgettable speech has one thread running all the way through it: The presenter is comfortable (even, perhaps, passionate) with what they are doing and it shows.

So, without getting all clever and scientific about it, three things to keep in mind:

- the more you work at it the better it will be
- you must be comfortable
- you need to take on and absorb the basics (ie everything we've covered so far)

Oh sure, there are some people who seem to be natural orators. You get the impression they could talk about anything (often do!) at the drop of a hat. But they are the very rare birds in a cage full of sparrows and you don't see their distinctive plumage or hear their voice too often.

I'll be giving you advice from some of these professionals later.

For the rest of us – and that's 99.99 percent of the world's adult population – there's the only other option: Work at it. There is nothing, nothing at all, like preparation. Knowing the script, the slide transitions, having a deep knowledge of the subject produce two things, comfort and confidence.

> **Susan Says**
> Here's where the written word and the spoken word differ sharply. You can edit and re-edit the written word right to the last minute. But the spoken word requires more time for the speaker to become comfortable with the flow. Don't edit/change the presentation until right before you give it or you never hit your comfort level.

One way to be comfortable is to make sure that you start your presentation with material that you feel confident about. By focusing on information that you know really well for the first few minutes should mean that you are nicely "in the groove". Whatever you do, do not begin with the part you know very little about. It may be hard to know everything about your topic (you may be very new in your job, for instance) so again, focus on the parts you feel the most confident and knowledgeable about.

And if you feel comfortable you will look like a true professional from the first time you open your mouth. Comfort at the lectern comes from feeling in control. And the reason you are in control is that you know the presentation backwards and forwards. Finally, a great deal of that comfort comes from the fact that you have checked all the boxes in building your presentation.

If you have done all that (and every step is described in the book), then you can begin to add some bells and whistles to make that speech really zing!

> **Susan Says**
> Whatever attention-getting tricks you decide to use, you need to add _value_ as well as interest. Make sure it's appropriate for you, your audience, and your message. Yes, be comfortable with it.

The AIMS! model describes how to package your message, beginning with getting both acceptance and interest from the audience. Here's something to keep in mind – if you don't gain the interest of the participants at the beginning, it's doubtful you'll have it at the end. So this part of the speech is very important.

John Scully, Managing Director of SPO Partners in San Francisco, a successful private equity firm, says that every speaker needs to learn the 'elevator pitch'. That's what he terms the short, to-the-point presentation that captures immediately the attention of busy people. Can you tell your story in the time an elevator takes to go from the ground floor to the top? If you can't do that, says Scully, in this busy world, don't be surprised if the audience brings out their BlackBerry's and start texting and emailing. Under the table, of course!

Most presentations are made up of three parts: openings, closings and the bits in the middle. My AIMS! model (see Chapter One) puts the opening and introduction on different levels, and breaks the closing into a "summary" and a "closing". If you're not already a world-class statesman, sports player, movie or rock star, chances are the audience won't be hanging on your every word from the beginning. Therefore, you need to attract and hold their attention. That's where great openings come in.

The Beginning

Remember – the "A" in AIMS! is for "Acceptance". The job of the opening is to make the audience have an emotional connection with you. You look for some common denominator that binds them to you. Beginning perhaps with phrases in their language (King Juan Carlos of Spain opening the Barcelona Olympics in Catalan – the language used by people in that area), or pointing out similar experiences, backgrounds, values, mentioning earlier meetings, linking to the theme of the meeting – all these can quickly establish your connection to that audience. It also shows that you know who they are. You would be surprised how many speakers start their presentation with no thought to how it should differ from group to group. And audiences figure this out very quickly.

Alternatively, you could start by grabbing their interest from the off, then go back to your common ground. That phrase "you never get a second chance to make a good first impression" is as true today as when Julius Caesar said it when he crossed the Rubicon in 49 BC.

No! Of course he didn't say it, but I got your attention – didn't I?

That's a perfect illustration of an opening based on securing "Interest" – the "I" in AIMS!. Something that grabs the attention of the audience. It lets you directly into their consciousness. Now all you have to do is stay there.

Openings and introductions come in many shapes and sizes. You can use evidence, facts, humour, topical references, geographic, historical, and current events; references to where you are, comments about the audience, explanation of how you will meet their needs, information on what you are going to tell them (history, status, future plans, problems, issues, opportunities and solutions). All these provide an opportunity to engage quickly and painlessly with an audience. A safe bet is to appeal to the WIIFM (What's In It For Me), that every audience has deep down it it's heart. If you can immediately show and explain what the value-added is for the audience, you are off to a really good start.

It's your choice how you begin a presentation, but the big idea to keep in mind is impact. If you can get their attention from the first moment you are a long way to satisfying their needs and putting your message across. Remember the Single Overriding Communication Objective (SOCO) in Chapter One? Well that is what should govern how you start. Mould your opening words to the thing you most want to get across to the audience. This can be done in a huge variety of ways. To get you started – and thinking – here are some of the possible approaches to the opening.

And to do this, you don't have to be as dramatic as Steve Ballmer, CEO of Microsoft, who began a company presentation running across the stage screaming loudly and finally yelling at the very top of his voice – "I LOVE THIS COMPANY!" For sure, no one forgot that opening. But that kind of drama is reserved for very few situations. That said, when you're the CEO of Microsoft you can probably darn well do anything you like!

Using evidence and facts

Susan Says
Beginning with "My name is (whatever)" is one of the most boring ways to start a presentation. Say something interesting first, then give your name if you haven't been introduced by anyone.

That old saying, "never let the facts get in the way of a good story" may have merit somewhere, but I've never subscribed to it. Quite the opposite. I find that facts – the truth – are usually stranger than fiction. There's nothing so compelling as a speaker reeling off a list of facts at the outset of a presentation – particularly those that grab the audience and get their immediate attention. Bigger, better, bizarre – all these things audiences just love to hear. And this works in almost every situation from global warming to the launch of a new sales campaign. Nobel prize-winner Al Gore isn't the only one who can scare the pants off an audience – you can too. Not only that, but you can bring it into the context of your audience, focusing them very quickly on what you are about to say.

Example: "I'm not going to talk about how global warming is threatening the planet. I'm going to tell you about what it means for Greentown. If we don't take action now, in 20 years we will have" (then list the horrors waiting to unfold).

Example: "Today, there are 150 million people over 60 in Europe. By 2015 there will be 175 million. It is to meet the needs of this ever-expanding age-group that we have created the XYZ service.

Using common ground, by referring to people or incidents the audience are familiar with is a good way to catch attention (and generally a fairly safe approach). Try to find out who you can mention in the beginning that the audience would recognize immediately, and start with those references. Many years ago, I worked with the legendary comedian Bob Hope on some live shows he did for various groups. No matter how many times he had done the show, he changed the routine to fit each audience; throwing out names (in the beginning and throughout the performance) of people the audience would recognize. Always the consummate professional, he never, ever took an audience for granted.

Using topical references

News holds our interest, so linking the opening of a presentation to a topical issue is a useful way of drawing the audience into what you have to say. And it doesn't have to be some comment about a global event. Indeed, topical, local stories often have a greater impact, especially if they bolster or frame your argument as they connect you directly to a local group.

Example: "So, the local school board has ignored our campaign for better facilities. But this just makes me more determined. Here's what I think we should do." Bring the newspaper or magazine with the article (or these days the YouTube cast), they always make a good prop.

Example: "Three new laws on product safety will be passed by the government in the next 12 months. Yes, they will affect our business. They also provide a unique opportunity for us to……"

If there are major sports competitions happening that relate to the audience, you can use these as well to begin. Historical references (the name of the street, the building or the room where you are, a close by monument, the historical significance of the day or the area) are always interesting to the audience when we tie them into the event and your presentation. Even linking to the conference or meeting theme is a great way to start and show common ground and interest.

Using the audience's expectations

Susan says
Pre-emptive disclosure is where you tell the audience up-front what you know is in their minds (even if the disclosure is a painful one). If you wait for the rumours or the objection you are sure to get from the audience, you will defend your message. If you introduce the disclosure first, you will control the message.

Unless you are living in a dictatorship (in which case keep this book hidden under your mattress!), audiences tend to come to an event of their own free will. The only exception to that is when the CEO makes his annual speech to the employees and it doesn't do to be absent (yes, you're right some organizations are a bit like Stalinist Russia). That means, it is a good idea to meet, exceed or – if you are very confident – challenge their expectations. Meet them and exceed them, especially if you agree with them and you'll quickly establish a mutual comfort zone. Challenge them and you will certainly be remembered!

Example: "I think you know why I am here today. Yes, to get you to join me in a journey to become one of the top performing companies in our industry. My role, is to tell you how we are going to make that happen."

Example: "You thought I was going to tell you about our award for excellence didn't you? Well, I am. But we didn't just win one, we won three!"

Example: "I've heard the rumours. You've heard the rumours. The truth is we have just bought the XYZ company. Yes, they're three times our size, but we are in the best position to exploit the market. So there's lots to do and let's get on with it!

Tell a story

It's not only fairy stories that begin "once upon a time," great presentations can too. Over the years I heard presenters use this opening to great effect. OK, it doesn't work if you want to arouse the audience or get them wound up and motivated, but if you want to operate in their comfort zone a story (true, I hope) can work really well. Having said that, I wouldn't try it with very large audiences as the intimacy can be all too easily lost.

Remember, all good stories explain the complex in simple terms or have a basic moral to them. They also have a happy ending. To tell a story that the audience can quickly engage with and believe in, you must set the scene quickly, populate the story with familiar characters (bad witches, dragons and demons for the competition perhaps) and draw it all to a successful conclusion.

I once heard a Dutch economist begin his presentation with "Once upon a time..." The entire audience waited expectantly (like children curled up ready for a bedtime story) for the rest of the narrative to unfold. He then proceeded to talk about old and new economics and continued to hold the audience spellbound. What a great start!

It is no accident that all religious leaders, throughout time, have transmitted their messages through stories. People tend to dislike speeches but they love stories, anecdotes or full blown sagas. That way, the audience wraps their minds around the story and holds on for the "happy" ending." Stories create images in the mind of the listener – and people are always very curious to hear how they end.

Using humour

While jokes (with punchlines) can be dangerous (the timing has to be right on the button), humour (a funny story or anecdote) can work well if it is presented in the right context and with the right delivery. But, what is considered funny varies widely from culture to culture, so make sure it adds to the value of the message and that the audience will understand the meaning.

Some presenters get away with using jokes to get the audience's attention no matter where they are. My view is that unless you are very confident and possess excellent timing it isn't something to play around with. All too often I have seen presenters come very quickly unstuck (never to recover) because of an attempt at humour that didn't work. There is no silence quite like the one when an audience doesn't laugh – it's like a vacuum. Think long and hard before you go down this route.

Shock the audience

Shocking an audience is to move them away from their comfort levels and has to be done with a great deal of precision and a lot of forethought. Think about it this way. Every audience, no matter where you go in the world, comes to a meeting with some preconceived ideas of what's going to happen. If you choose to blow that bubble of expectation you really need to know why you are doing that and have worked out what kind of reaction it will set off. People tend to be traditional animals and taking them out of their comfort context can be a dangerous thing to play around with.

However, if you think that it is something you can pull off, shocking an audience certainly grabs their attention.

Example: "Sales figures? I'm not going to talk about them. Why would I? My concern is, will we be in business next month?" That guarantees 100 percent attention from everyone – forever.

Example: "I really appreciate this invitation to talk to you today. Maybe if you knew what I was going to say you wouldn't have asked me, but, I guess it's too late now." You have said nothing yet, but they know that something is about to happen. You have their full attention. If you have a streak of cruelty in you it is possible to draw out the "anticipation" of the shock to come for several minutes!

Reinout Van Lennep, the ABN AMRO executive I mentioned earlier, started a scheduled 20-minute presentation to a leadership group by saying "If you think I came all the way to Frankfurt from Zurich for a 20-minute talk, you're *wrong*. I plan to stay for the next two hours to talk about leadership." He received a standing ovation at the end. Naturally, the program planners knew he was going to use more time!

One of the best I ever heard came from a tough talking American CEO. In front of the assembled company after a day of enforced firings he got to his feet and said, "Those of you in this room have not been let go, if you look around I'm sure you'll see who's missing." Not diplomatic, but attention-getting yes!

Telling them what they will go away with

I think it's always a good idea to tell an audience what you are going to tell them. It paves the way for what's to come. It also allows you to build up anticipation and get your key message across right at the beginning. Audiences usually feel good about knowing from the outset what's in store for them. In reality, telling them what they are going to take away from the session means that they can order it all in their own minds, checking mental boxes as you work your way through the list.

Susan Says

I always feel that in the majority of cases, people want to like you. They empathize with you up there on the stage. They want you to be interesting and fire their enthusiasm. Don't start out with that "will they like me?" attitude, that isn't going to help.

Moreover, I find that most people like the idea of getting something, learning something, especially if you can make them feel they are being given something new that others haven't heard yet. Being the first to know is always a powerful potion that works on all kinds of groups. And of course, always stress What's In It For Them!

Using props

We get into some detail about the use of props in Chapter Six, but there is no doubt that they can have a place in an opening (or the middle for that matter) to create some drama or surprise. Obviously it depends on the place and the context of the presentation as to what kind of materials you might want to use, but something that rivets the attentions or makes people relax is always worthwhile. Again, timing is important. So if you can't get it right every time, don't try it.

Apple's Steve Jobs uses props beautifully in his media shows where he pulls a tiny iPhone out of his pocket or an incredibly thin MacBook Air computer out of a small envelope. To talk about the product without creating this magical experience with the device would not have been as effective. Then again, how many millions of dollars did it take, and how many technicians to make it happen? You may not be Steve Jobs, but you can be innovative too. A Rubik's cube to show how complicated something is or a newspaper with a current related article are two simple examples of props that put some *wow* into your presentation.

How not to open

There's one thing no one must ever do – apologize!

I've seen so many presentations flounder just because the speaker has apologized at the very outset. Phrases like, "I've never made this presentation before....", or "I was only asked last night to stand in for Bill...", don't garner sympathy. They just make you look ill-prepared, unprofessional and silly.

Susan says
Always know exactly - to the point of nerdiness - how you will open (the brain is on automatic pilot at this moment). That way, you start and stay in control.

Now, as I said earlier, there is nothing wrong with clarifying that the presentation you are about to give is not your own – just don't apologize for the fact. Neither should you forget what I said earlier, don't take on a presentation if you don't feel comfortable with the role or able to fulfil it to the point where you look good and achieve your objectives.

Make sure that your notes are in order and that you are ready when you are announced. Stop, look at your audience, pause, then move to that well rehearsed opening. Don't mumble or fumble. Show that you are in charge.

The Summary and Closing – or the Grand Finale!

Never end with problems – always provide some kind of solution. No audience on earth wants to leave feeling down or discouraged. Your job is to make sure they leave informed, refreshed, even uplifted. Make sure you always end on a positive note. Even if you are the bearer of bad news give them at least a fleeting glimpse of the light at the end of the tunnel. Try to find a phrase or a short anecdote that neatly sums up your message. Giving an audience something they can take away with them ensures you are remembered long after the session is over.

Always, always, always remember at the end to "tell them what you have told them." Repetition is important if you want people to remember your message. And don't make it too long. A summary should be just that. Ideally break it down to just a few key bullet points that sum up everything that has gone before.

The call to action

A good way to make sure that the audience doesn't leave feeling that you're hit them with an insoluble problem is to leave them with a few "here's what you can do" tips. As you close suggest that there are several things that they now need to do that will help them when they get back to the office.

Example: "When you get to the office tomorrow morning, here are three things you can do that will really improve how you look at this issue (list the three things)."

Example: "Before you go, let me leave you with two things you can try that will help you……"

Example: "While you're getting ready for work tomorrow, play these three things over in your mind. They'll make you think a lot differently about your day."

Make sure your audience understands *exactly* what you want them to do, who should do it, and when. How much will the recommendation cost, whose budget will it come from, and how will the resources be used. Vague next actions may result in no next actions.

Make them want more

The really smart professional presenters do this all the time – leave the audience wanting more of them. While it isn't an easy trick to pull off it does mean that they will remember you long after the others are forgotten. Give them just enough to get the message across, but not all of the answers. Leave them still thinking about what happens next.

The closing that gets them to leave the theatre whistling – this is the "!!!" in the AIMS! model.

Susan Says

Audience attention peaks at the beginning and the end of a presentation. These are the times to reinforce your key messages. The closing allows you to inspire the listeners to do something. Unlike the summary, where you told them what to do next, the closing makes them want to do it

If you have had a lengthy question and answer session following your presentation, you may want to revisit your "next step" summary before moving to your closing. The audience may have forgotten what you wanted them to do.

I often use what I call "the red line" by reminding them of something I told them in the beginning and then referring to it again in the end.

Other ways of keeping an audience's attention:

- Tell a story that inspires the audience to believe what you want them to do can be done. A story about people (much like themselves) who have successfully done what you are proposing.

- Empower your audience. If you want your factory workers to invest more time in quality control or safety measures, your closing story could cite a real example about a vigilant employee who caught a serious error or avoided an accident by applying your ideas and advice.

- Quotations make great closings. I heard a speaker who wanted senior management to make changes to deal with a volatile market. She used a Chinese proverb "We cannot direct the wind, but we can adjust the sail."

- Challenge them! I like Nike's short challenge – Just do it! Also, Kofi Annan, then secretary general of the UN, closed a speech at an international conference by issuing a challenge: "The people of Afghanistan have a hard road ahead of them. Let us not leave them to travel it alone."

- Finally, a simple closing is The Headline. Like a newspaper heading, the headline makes the message very clear in one or two lines. I signal I am closing by saying something like "I want to leave you with one important message" and then I deliver the "headline" or key point I want them to remember.

How not to close

You might think that the toughest part of speech-making is getting started, often it's the other way around. The end can be fraught with dangers if not tackled in the right way. And a bad ending is such a waste. All that hard work for what? So an audience can see you get it wrong at the end?

However, a great many would-be presenters put all their effort into that wonderful, not-to-be-forgotten opening and the main body of the delivery and somehow forget that eventually (just like all good things) you need to wind it up.

Apart from never, never, ending with "thank you for listening" or "thank you for your attention", here are four things you need to avoid:

The spluttering halt

This happens when you are just not prepared to end. You literally run out of material – usually too early. This leaves you looking lost and uncertain, and you are also in good company as the audience and any chairperson are in the same boat with you. Once you've lost it like that there's nothing much to be pulled back. You've lost your authority and your message has just gone up in smoke amid the embarrassing silence. This is one reason why it is vital to time your presentation.

Emergency stop

The other reason to check the length is to avoid the "emergency stop." This is when a speaker suddenly realizes that they are at the end of their time slot and just stop. So there is no time for a conclusion or a summary or those last few memorable words. Like the splutter, the emergency stop leaves your would-be message hanging limply in the air – not the impression you wanted to leave.

Remember: time the thing!

Run over time and get thrown off

Just as bad, or possibly worse is getting thrown off the stage. Trouble is, if that happens you probably deserved it. These are the presenters who ignore agreed time slots and just do it their way. Often – because many conference chairmen are not too vigilant – they get away with it. But again, when someone pulls the plug it is embarrassing and it is the only part of your hour of fame that the people listening will ever remember about you. Make sure it doesn't happen. Be punctual – it pays.

Susan Says

Two things here. First, put your watch or small clock on the lectern and check it from time to time. Second, if there is a chairperson, ask them to give you a ten- and a five-minute sign. I always use a small digital clock that I can easily see and I pace myself so that I always know where I should be during the presentation. If you do run out of time, the part of the presentation you do __not__ cut is the closing. Rehearsing and timing your material in advance will help you avoid these pitfalls.

Can't wrap it up

I term this "the never ending story." This is where a speaker can't find the way to stop (often nerves drive them onwards) and just keeps on going. Phrases like, "let me remind you," and "to mention once again" just keep coming up. Understandably the audience gets nervous too, shifting and shuffling they have long lost the will to listen, never mind remember what it was all about in the first place.

Now the Stuff in Between – Otherwise Known as the Message

I call this part the meat in the sandwich. And just like the filling in a crusty roll it can be bland or it can be added to – a few pickles or chillies never did any harm to a sandwich and they won't to a speech either.

The meat in the middle is the M for Message in the AIMS! Model. This part is also called the danger zone – or Death Valley – in terms of attention. Audiences always need a lot of help staying tuned in for this – the core of the message. The thing to remember is that if you have an opening packed with power and promise and an ending equally erudite and exciting, then you can't very well have something limp squashed unthinkingly between those two bright moments.

Start as you mean to go on has never been sounder advice. You need to make sure that you keep up the pace and prolong the attention of the people in front of you. While I go into a great amount of detail throughout the book, do remember that writing a smart opening and ending is not enough. You must make sure that the whole process has pace, punch and that you deliver it with presence. OK, some presentations are more serious than others, that doesn't matter, the basic rules of creating something that does the job it sets out to do must always apply. And that goes for the main body of the speech. Openings and endings don't make a speech. They are the frame to hold it in place, but the whole structure has to be sound to make it work.

Stir them up with the opening. Settle them down with the content and then send them off with a resounding memory in their heads. Just remember how to stop!

Make the middle memorable

First be sure you that have no more than three major topics. People won't remember much more, so focus on three key messages. For each new audience, change your examples and the evidence that support your topics.

For instance, if your audience is interested in the "numbers", provide that as evidence of your argument. On the other hand, human resource professionals might be more interested in productivity and people-related examples. People want to be able to associate with the information, and examples help you tailor your message to their reality. If I speak in Asia, I use Asian examples, etc. Use phrases and terms from their business or industry to explain concepts. Quote people who are well known and respected by that audience.

In training, the examples become demonstrations and then exercises where everyone participates.

Consider areas where you might bring something special to the presentation. I have seen presenters who were scuba divers use great photos they had taken of sharks to liven up PowerPoint slides about the competition. Chess players make excellent use of the key points of the game to outline strategic planning. And football fans (whether it is the US or European version) can motivate teams by using that game's tactics, making comparisons along the way.

I have seen technicians who happened to be magicians make technical presentations come alive by using tricks. People who can draw can use flip charts to make points and not rely on PowerPoint all the time.

The people I have mentioned learned that they could use their personal enthusiasm to help get their message across and it worked. It worked because the extra effort they took to make the information come alive not only captured and kept the audience interest, but it added value – and often passion – to the message.

Topping and Tailing

Another point about openings and closings needs to be made. For anyone who has to give the same presentation over and over again (and there are many people in that position), you can make even the best delivery better by creating new opening and closing sections.

What this means is you can have a central core that hardly varies (and you can get to know really, really well), but you adapt your beginnings and endings to suit the audience you have to reach.

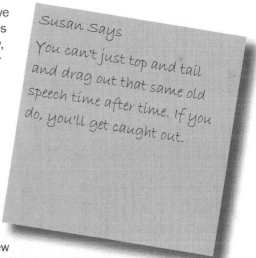

Susan Says

You can't just top and tail and drag out that same old speech time after time. If you do, you'll get caught out.

Wrapping a well-honed presentation with short starts and endings breathes new life into a presentation and makes the audience feel you are talking specifically to them – one of the keys to getting them on your side from the outset. Make sure you add new examples and evidence that are updated and relevant to the audience.

I know many professional speakers who have a core of five or six keynote speeches that they stick with (updating and revising a few minutes each year perhaps), but craft new pieces to meet different audience needs.

Do this, and your content will always seem fresh, to the point and, most important, relevant to the group you are addressing.

Wrapping Up For the Second Time

I've seen many presenters do a wonderful job – great opening, great message content and a great close, only to come unstuck when they think it's all over. Remember, it isn't over until you leave the platform.

For example, if you are asked to take questions, or join a panel on the platform, your core message can get easily forgotten. So try and do a short close when everything winds up. If you are unsure what's going to happen, choose a moment when you think things are winding down and say, "I'd just like to make a couple of key points here." Similarly, if you are answering questions on your own, take a last minute to stop the question and repeat your core message points.

Don't forget to do this. If things have gone really well (or even if they haven't) it's easy to get caught up in the thrill of the moment and just sit down. Presenters who do this a lot have their own little short wind-up piece that they can deliver in less than a minute. Less than a minute for something that audience participants will still recall weeks later.

Final Reminders

I hope I have made you appreciate just how important those openings and closings can be. Not to detract from the message, but to set up the presentation to get the message across in the very best way possible. However, it is important to stress that those that do this best really have worked and worked on their content and style. They know these things backwards – nothing less than an earthquake would put them off their stride (even then they'd still be talking as they ran for safety).

Chances are if you are reading this you're not in that league yet. No matter, you can deliver a very powerful performance just by making certain that you have all the points covered. That great opening will need work to get right, the main body of the delivery will need to be well rehearsed and the close must never, ever be overlooked.

Getting the whole presentation into line and delivering it to an approving audience is, I think, one of those great moments, whether it is in your professional or personal life. It's one of those things you have done, that stand out as a milestone.

Just never forget one thing, the harder you work at it the greater the payback will be. The day you feel comfortable on that platform is the day you'll know you've made it. The great thing is the audience will know that too!

Chapter 5

Mind Your Language!

"England and America are two countries divided by a common language."

George Bernard Shaw

**"Speak the speech, I pray you, as I pronounced it to you
– trippingly on the tongue."**

William Shakespeare

We live in an increasingly global world. More than that a great many of us work for or with major organizations in the private or public sector that operate all over the world.

> Susan says
> The trick to being successful with different cultures is to become a detective again. Find out about the culture and language levels of your audience so that you prepare material they will fully relate to and understand. Learn the do's and don'ts for the culture.

Therefore, it isn't an exaggeration to imagine that most of us will find ourselves at some point addressing an audience made up of a wide mix of nationalities, many of whom won't have English as their first, or possibly even second, language. Much of the work I have done over the years has involved working with multicultural teams and that has certainly brought its own rewards. There is something especially gratifying about seeing a group of very different people building each others' confidence to stand up and make a presentation (very often not in their mother tongue). At this point, presenting almost becomes secondary to the team building and other interpersonal skills that are created and developed.

However, whether you are facing a multinational mix at a global conference, or just addressing your European sales convention, there are – as always – some major do's and don'ts if you want to earn the plaudits of the audience.

What this chapter is all about is giving you some guidelines that you can follow, as well as some tips from my own experiences and some anecdotes from others I have seen and heard over the years. The intention is to give you enough information so you can adapt quickly and confidently to any situation that arises, wherever you are.

Keep it Simple

Here I go again with that phrase "keep it simple." But it is especially important when you have a mixed audience. Complex explanations and obscure charts and graphs won't sell your message. If you want to get that message across make sure that you emphasize just one or two key points that people can take away with them. This means:

- No difficult words. Otherwise you will lose people as they try and make sense of what you are saying

- No technical jargon. There's a good chance they won't know it. If you must use it, be sure to explain it.

- No acronyms. The audience is unlikely to belong to your "club" so don't make it even more difficult for them. This is also a good point to keep in mind in any presentation that is outside your immediate work or interest group.

- Don't use examples based on experiences or things that the audience has absolutely no knowledge of (you'd be surprised how many people make this mistake, usually due to misplaced enthusiasm!).

Susan Says
You can't connect with an audience if they don't know what you are talking about. Too often Americans use sports terminology garnered from baseball, football and basketball; the English attempt to liven up their delivery with cricketing terms. Advice! It doesn't work. All you do is lose the audience.

Look for examples in your message that are culturally targeted to the group you are talking to. I once spoke in Singapore to an audience of Asian private banking clients. I made a special effort to include Asian examples throughout the presentation. I kept many American and European examples that were relevant as well, but added the anecdotes that were related to people from that part of the world. My PowerPoint visuals were full of pictures of Asian – not just Western – speakers.

Remember the SOCO and Use It!

Yes! It's the SOCO again. Now just as important as before. What do you want to tell these people? How are you going to get it across? Advice: spend time thinking about this and how best to do it. Don't just do it the way you would on your home ground. Put yourself into the audience's shoes and think, "how will I come across, what is the most effective way to reach them? Then look for the kinds of examples I mentioned earlier.

You've got to keep in mind that the audience may be struggling to keep up with you and what you are saying. Make allowances for that and make certain your delivery is as clear and measured as you can make it.

Susan Says
One thing I've noticed over the years is that at any event where there is simultaneous translation a lot of the people who should be listening on their earphones to their mother tongue don't. Why? I've come to the conclusion that it's an ego thing – and possibly macho too! So be aware that there may be a large part of the audience that isn't really following you at all. There really isn't much you can do about this. Most interestingly though, the more senior the audience the more people are likely to do it.

Slow Down

Many of us, particularly if we are at all nervous, have the habit of speeding up our delivery. Really, really try to keep a nice pace. To audiences that may have difficulty following your presentation speak at least 20 percent more slowly than usual. This is hard to do. My thought on this? If you can, try to have a colleague in the audience signal you if you are talking too fast. And don't forget to *enunciate*. Poor word articulation isn't good anywhere, but it is especially confusing to people who do not speak or understand your language particularly well. And, another tip, speak in short sentences – not long ones – where possible.

WARNING! Be Careful When Speaking the Foreign Stuff!

Rock stars and famous politicians often use a few words of the local language at the beginning of a speech or an introduction. It can work for you as well, but only if you really practice the pronunciation and are sure those are the right words to use. But it can also be dangerous and you can end up saying something completely foolish or, worse still, insulting. Equally, avoid geographic references and the like unless you are totally sure of your ground.

The late, great James Hayes, the former head of the American Management Association and one of the world's outstanding speakers on business, is forever remembered in Portugal for getting to his feet in front of 200 top Portuguese managers and saying, "it's wonderful to be back here in Lisbon, Spain." The Portuguese and the Spanish have not liked sharing the Iberian Peninsula for hundreds of years. Jim's declaration pretty much blew his chances of acceptance – the "A" of AIMS! – right there!

You can certainly sympathize with speakers who are jet-lagged or tired and make verbal mistakes and unfortunate gaffes. I have seen and heard so many politicians on political campaigns speaking in numerous locations throughout the day, who simply forgot which town they were in. Unfortunate, yes, but not a disaster if you let the audience know later that you know who *they* are (even if you are not sure where *you* are).

Don't Sound Like a Zombie

Just because you need to keep it simple in situations like this doesn't mean you need to talk in words of three syllables or less. Don't make yourself sound stupid. Most importantly, don't talk down to the audience, not only will they be insulted they certainly won't buy your argument.

What I try to do (as I pointed out already in Chapter Three) is to get as much information about the group I will be talking to before I start. That way I can pitch the delivery somewhere just below the middle of the group's experience.

Be Friendly

Unless your job is to give out bad news, I always suggest that speakers in these situations go out of their way to be extra friendly. This makes the audience feel at ease and makes you look less like some alien being that has been parachuted into their world. Reaching out in this way seems to pay off and it helps your message to stick in their minds. You may be different, but at least you were nice to the locals. And that's the way to be.

Summaries In Their Language

Unless it is something very, very complex, a short (one page) summary of the key points of your presentation in the main languages the audience speak is a useful leave behind. Only point I would make here is make sure you have the translation checked by a native speaker. Over the years I have seen some absolute howlers. Believe me there are as many silly translations *from* English as there are into it.

Watch Cultural / Political Sensibilities

As I warned above, steer clear of trouble. Keep to your subject and don't deviate. Around the world there are enough problems for any accident-prone speaker to get quickly up to his or her neck in controversy. The rule is, "stick to what you know." It's all too easy not to just alienate but enrage an audience. Former vice president Dan Quayle's oft used blooper, "I wish I'd studied Latin at school, so I could talk to these Latin American people," might be funny, but it's amazing how many of us – in the stress of the moment can deliver something equally blundering.

It's said that when he attended the funeral of Charles De Gaulle, Richard Nixon declared "This is a great day for France". We may smile today and say, "how could he do that?" but, I bet, if someone followed any of us around with a microphone for 24 hours, most of us would be caught saying something we wish we hadn't.

Also, attacking another person's values rarely works and creates defensiveness in the listener. Your original SOCO could be lost in the ensuing verbal battle.

No Jokes Please

Jokes shouldn't be on the menu either. Unless you have the timing of a stand-up comic, you are just asking for trouble. Worse still, jokes don't travel well from culture to culture or country to country. For that matter they don't go from region to region either. What's funny in one country or one society can be either plain rude or completely unacceptable in another.

Still, it never ceases to amaze me how many presenters fail to see the danger and plunge in where angels and good manners fear to tread. As I've pointed out already, there is nothing more unnerving than the silence that follows an attempt at humour that the audience doesn't understand.

Susan Says

Leave any attempts at jokes for the cozy chat when it's all over and you're not trying to get your message across. A few jokes over a drink at the bar is one thing, an attempt to make an audience laugh is quite another.

Don't Try and Be Clever

This might seem to be self-evident, but it's surprising how many people manage to come across as somehow superior or arrogant. This is even easier to do when addressing international audiences, who seem to pick up certain nuances and behaviours in different ways. As with consciously keeping things simple and to the point, try not to talk down to people. Sure speak slowly, but don't make things so simple that it looks like you are addressing a class of five year-olds. Similarly, don't try and show how smart you are, the audience won't appreciate that either. One work colleague of mine once said that she always tried to be more like herself. While that may sound strange, I understand what she means. Think about how you want to be perceived and make sure that this is what comes across to the audience – in a natural way.

The April Fool's on You

A great illustration of how to be just too clever came at a conference some years ago where two presenters decided to play a joke on the audience. It was April 1st, which in some countries and cultures is celebrated as April Fool's Day. What happens is that people try and "fool" other people, most often into believing that something outrageous or silly is really true.

At the conference, which had a huge mix of nationalities, the speaker got up and presented a "case study" of a so-called famous management thinker. The truth was the speaker had made the whole thing up. As he spoke (he had illustrations and slides to back up the story) the facts and the whole story become more and more bizarre. While about 80 percent of the audience eventually got the joke, many didn't. They were eagerly taking notes. At the end, people in the audience were asking where they could buy this "guru's" books. When it was explained that the person didn't exist they just didn't get the joke!

Translators and Interpreters

I am continuously amazed at how few speakers (even those who have been treading conference platforms for many years) seem to take any notice of the simultaneous interpreters at major events. These people are, in reality, your voice. They are taking what you say and "translating" it for the audience. So, if you want to get your message across, doesn't it make sense to help these professionals do the best job they can? Their best job translates into the best job of getting your ideas across in another language.

Interpreters are highly skilled, but always seem to be underestimated, if they are noticed at all. Where I find myself at a conference or event with simultaneous or sequential translation, I always make a point of going to see the interpreters and having a chat. Usually, I try and catch them early during a break in the event and take the opportunity not only to introduce myself but to tell them about my presentation. I've found that taking this time is not only greatly appreciated by them, but also means that they are going to pay a lot more attention to my session. Bring written material with explanations of terms to give them in advance. Make sure they understand your message *before* you speak through them.

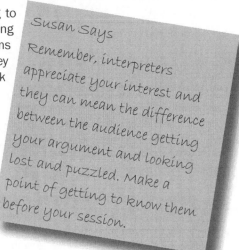

Susan Says

Remember, interpreters appreciate your interest and they can mean the difference between the audience getting your argument and looking lost and puzzled. Make a point of getting to know them before your session.

This can be particularly important if you have a complex presentation or want to specifically emphasize some points.

As one of my colleagues once explained to me, there's another reason for being nice to the interpreters, "you have no idea what they are saying you are talking about!" Yes, be friendly, its much better that way.

Speaking in a Second Language: English

There used to be a sort of unwritten rule that unless you were completely fluent in a second language you should avoid speaking it in public. However, the increased globalization of our world means two things: first, the de facto language of business is English and, second, more and more non-native English speakers are having to use the language as their primary means of communication. This extends to presentations too.

My advice is very straightforward on this. If you are not English mother-tongue there is one thing you need to do: rehearse, rehearse, rehearse. If you think it is hard for a native English speaker it is doubly hard for someone with another language to contend with.

Therefore, if you're reading this book because you have a presentation to make in English but it isn't your first language, there are two things you must do:

● Get your presentation ready as early as you can, so that you are familiar with all facets of it

● Rehearse it at every opportunity you get. Make sure you have someone with English as their mother-tongue to help you wherever possible.

Let me give you some examples or why being well prepared and rehearsing is important.

One future European president for a major US corporation, whose mother tongue was Spanish, was smart enough to use a professional speechwriter (see Chapter Twelve) from the beginning. Once the theme of the presentation was agreed, the writer would put a complete script together and he would take it with him everywhere he went. By the time it came for him to get on the platform, he was not only word perfect but he had every nuance and emphasis down pat. Indeed, he was so impressive, that he outshone his English-speaking colleagues who probably didn't take the time to get it right. Another point, to drive home how good he was (still is, I should say – he later became the president of the firm), he never used notes in the final presentations. That doesn't mean using notes is a bad thing, but it does indicate the less the speaker looks like he or she needs prompting, the better.

Another example of getting it right was a Polish engineer who was put in charge of a major locomotive plant by his new French bosses. His English wasn't too good. He was all right talking about the finer points of an engineering blueprint or looking at the snags in a production line, but that was about it. Trouble was the senior executives in Paris wanted him to present to a company-wide get-together of 500 plus managers and engineers.

Faced with this challenge, our Polish engineer opted for the same approach – he hired a professional. In this case it was an intensive series of sessions (the presentation was two weeks away). The writer and coach moved into the locomotive plant for a week and just kept working on him. By the end of the first week he was word perfect. By mid-way through the second week he knew what the words meant too!

Susan says
If there are words in a language that are difficult for you to say, find another word that means the same thing and is easier for you to pronounce. Or keep practising the word until you get it right.

The big day came and he was sensational! Not only because it all made sense and was delivered so well, but just that this ugly duckling of an engineer had turned into a confident, professional swan of a presenter. Luckily he remembered the next rule in situations like this – don't ask for questions!

You'll find more on the importance of rehearsals in Chapter Eleven.

A leading French business school professor quietly counsels, "if you are French and speaking in English don't ever, ever, use the word 'focus.'" Think about it! This is sound advice. Words don't always work right (or sound right) when you try and use them in the heat of a presentation. Tongues really do get twisted.

One of my memories is of an international leadership conference with a French-speaking chairperson. It was very international, with many nationalities, including a large contingent from the Arab world. On the morning of the first day the chairperson delivered her opening address and startled many in the audience with her passionate plea for "getting rid of all Iraqis." This we thought a bit extreme. It was only after she had repeated this threat several times to the evident discomfort of parts of the audience that we realized she was trying to say, "getting rid of all *hierarchies*!" Just a little different.

Sadly, it is a cruel world out there when it comes to speaking in public. The French drop their Hs and the Chinese turn Rs into Ls. Those of us lucky enough to have English as a mother-tongue, the language that is the preferred one for global communication, should be forever thankful. Not only that, we should treat our language with respect – as those who don't have it as their native speech most often do – and learn to use it to the very best of our ability.

Speaking in a Second Language: Non-English

As far as I am concerned, the same rules apply for any of us English speakers tackling a foreign language – be careful, be prepared, be very well rehearsed. My instinct is to advise you that if you have any doubts at all – any – just say "no."

If you feel you are not capable of giving an entire speech in a second (or third) language, practice really well a few words you can use in the opening to show the audience you took the time to "speak their language." If you are really uncomfortable in another language, a simple "good morning" or "thank you" in their tongue will do.

Susan Says

The written word and the spoken word are very different. The written word must be as correct as possible. Have a native speaker check your handouts and slides (it is incredible how many smart, intelligent senior-level people fail to do this).

Test, Test, Test

Finally, don't put a speech together all on your own. Try it out and test drive it with someone else. Get their thoughts and views. Make sure they sit right through it and have someone who's not afraid to criticize the content, style and technique. Having an "audience" to present to before an event helps build confidence and correct any flaws before the real targets get to hear and see you. One other thing, I guarantee if you rehearse with a colleague, you'll make at least one significant change in your presentation.

The Gender Issue

When we talk about minding your language, I cannot avoid discussing some issues related to different genders in an audience. Just as you must be sensitive to saying things that disturb or cause defensiveness in cultures or nationalities, the same is true for references to men and women.

I don't know why, but women are often held to different standards than men, particularly about using certain kinds of language or off-colour humour. Simply put, don't try, it rarely works. Men too should be cautious about using certain words: like "chairman" or "salesmen", which could indicate (depending on your audience) that only men can chair or sell in an organization. No need to be paranoid about this, but do be careful that your language and examples are balanced in terms of culture, race, and gender. A couple of minutes to look through your presentation and weed out any potential no-no's are all it takes. And this is another good reason to rehearse on colleagues before the presentation – they will hear and pick up on potentially dangerous words and phrases that you may not.

Now, let's move on to Chapter Six and, having got the presentation right (you have, haven't you?), consider the kind of visuals we may want to add to make the delivery more exciting.

Chapter 6

Visuals – a Boon or a Bane?

"The phrase 'Death by PowerPoint' is common corporate parlance."

Jared Sandberg, The Wall Street Journal

"One Picture is Worth Ten Thousand Words"

Chinese proverb

All too often I see smart individuals who, when asked to prepare a presentation, click immediately on the PowerPoint icon on their desktop. Sorry to say, this knee-jerk reaction is *not* the way to do it. One of the biggest mistakes I see would-be speakers make is structuring their presentation based on PowerPoint instead of the other way around. Begin with your message outline, *then* – and only then – identify slides that will help you get that message across.

You may need no slides or you may need lots, but base your use of PowerPoint on the structure you have designed from the outset.

What?! No PowerPoint?

Today, most companies seem to expect to be zapped with a glittering array of PowerPoint in every presentation, whether it's needed or not. So prevalent can this get inside a business that Nokia's headquarters in Finland are even nicknamed "PowerPoint Palace" by the many of the people who work there.

But despite – or more likely because of – the all pervasive use of PowerPoint, good presenters as well as many senior managers, know that we are getting "PowerPoint Poisoning," and something needs to be done about it. But just what's the solution when everyone's a "user"; everyone has been injected with the same corporate drug? Well, to borrow a phrase from another campaign, my thought is to "Just Say No."

The Slides are the Handouts

Another reason people reach for the PowerPoint is that slides are very often used as handouts and not always projected. Because of that, ridiculous amounts of detail go into the slides to explain them to the reader. Norbert Barnich, a PowerPoint expert who spent years at Management Centre Europe in Brussels helping speakers improve their visuals, describes the handout use of PowerPoint as being like the book you read, versus the projected slide show, which is the movie version. As he advises, "Don't try to make the audience read the book on the movie screen." Put the details into Speakers Notes in PowerPoint and reduce the amount of text and graphics on the actual slide. You'll be glad you did – more than that, so will the audience!

But How Will I Remember What I Want to Say?

Speakers – especially lazy speakers – rely on the security blanket of PowerPoint to jog their memory at every turn – or rather click of the mouse. Yes, the slides can help guide you through your presentation, but don't subject the audience to material on the screen that serves no other purpose than to remind you what you wanted to say. It all comes across as just a bit haphazard and very unprofessional. Solution? Make separate notes if you need to. Better solution? Rehearse!

The Case for No Visuals At All

Some of the most powerful, moving and long-remembered presentations I have seen and heard in my professional career have had no visuals at all. Perhaps that's because there's nothing more powerful than a lone individual delivering a heartfelt speech – something that they clearly believe in and want the audience to believe in too. Picture a fired-up Barack Obama, running for the US presidency, standing on the stage with PowerPoint. No way! Even this man who loves his gadgets and technology – did not rely on slides to talk his way to the presidency.

Do you remember that Dilbert cartoon "PowerPoint poisoning"? The one where a member of the audience keels over as Dilbert is saying "As you can clearly see in slide 397". That's what you have to avoid!

Of course presentations like this are usually memorable because there are very few people who can pull them off. And that really sets me up for the next piece of advice. Most people – although they rarely admit it, even to themselves – use visuals as a crutch, a support. They sort of hide in the corner and let the visuals talk for them. Or, as I said earlier, lazy presenters use them as an aide memoir and a security blanket they can wrap around themselves. This isn't a good idea. Why? Because if you want to sell anything, inform people of anything, get their attention and enthusiasm, it is *you* who have to do it. It is all about you. All the fancy slides in the world won't help if you – personally – can't connect with that audience.

Enough!

Management in many companies I know have started limiting slides to between three and five per presentation. So what do nervous, unrehearsed speakers do in response? They pack twenty slides-worth of data into the permitted three or five. Result? No one can understand anything at all!

And so, we have Death by PowerPoint. It's not Microsoft's fault that people abuse it badly, instead of use it well. In fact the software is a great tool when it's used correctly. So let's look at how you can exploit the tool to enhance your presentation (as it was originally designed to do).

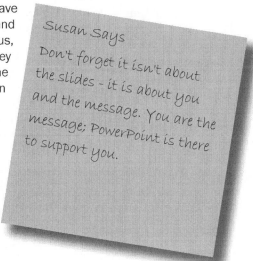

Susan Says

Don't forget it isn't about the slides – it is about you and the message. You are the message; PowerPoint is there to support you.

When to Use PowerPoint

The time for PowerPoint is when you can show and explain points in your presentation better if people can see them and not just hear them. Slides must add value for the audience, not just to you. You can show your audience places and faces they could not understand as well without seeing them. You can build up information slowly – in layers – so that people comprehend complex material more easily. You can visually highlight information you believe is extremely important. And when PowerPoint does all of this, it is a remarkably effective information tool – that can make us better presenters, not worse.

For my money, there are only really two good reasons for having visuals in a presentation:

- they add and enhance to the story you are telling
- they make your story more exciting and more meaningful

If they are not going to do that, why are you staring at that PowerPoint screen?

How do I begin?

To get to the stage where PowerPoint is working for you, not the other way around, keep your SOCO in mind and look at your AIMS! outline with the Post-its (Chapter One). The outline you have created already has the basic structure and it can now be evolved to include visuals.

How do we do that? By taking smaller Post-its or just making marks on square Post-its indicating where you think slides could go to add value to your message.

Amazingly, when I ask people to do this in a seminar, they are always shocked at how few slides they really need to make their point. Often they have arrived with a large file of PowerPoint slides, only to select or develop a small percentage of the amount they thought they would need.

You may remember the sample AIMS! chart we used in Chapter One. Here is the chart again, but with small squares that show where, once the message is developed, slides might be used to enhance the presentation. Note that in this sample, I chose not to use slides in my opening (where I establish acceptance from the audience on a personal level) nor in the closing. You may choose to add more (or fewer) slides. Just base your decisions on how much the slide adds value to your message.

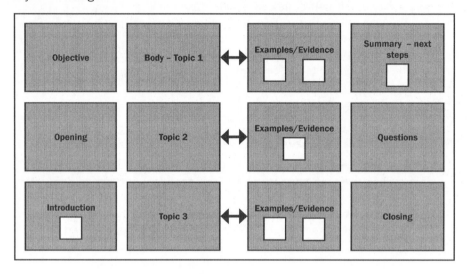

Now that you have created your basic structure for the presentation and identified places where slides should go, take a piece of paper – yes paper – and begin with that. Use a pencil so you can rub things out (more fun and less time consuming than pointing, dragging and clicking, believe me!). Take a letter size or A4 sheet, and divide it into four quadrants. Turn it around so that it is longer than it is tall ("landscape"). Each quadrant represents about the amount of space you have to design a clear, viewable slide (still using your pencil). Can't put much there, can you? Well, that tells you something about how much we are trying to put onto a single slide.

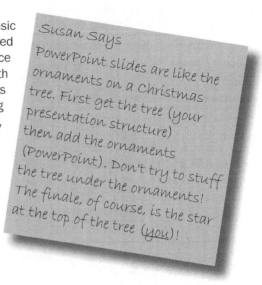

Susan Says

PowerPoint slides are like the ornaments on a Christmas tree. First get the tree (your presentation structure) then add the ornaments (PowerPoint). Don't try to stuff the tree under the ornaments! The finale, of course, is the star at the top of the tree (you)!

OK, I know that you won't use the pencil and paper method for long, since it is so much easier to go directly to a PowerPoint slide, but designing one visual by hand gives you an idea about how much information we can really put on that screen. The answer is, you don't want much!

The Good, the Bad and the Awful

In my years of teaching people how to present I've seen and heard just about everything you can imagine (and some things you can't) that people think they can get away with. It is quite amazing just how much effort people can put into making a mess of things.

What you don't want to do is turn people off. But that's what happens when you take yourself out of the picture and put those slides in your place. So here are some of the things you need to think about when it comes to letting visuals enhance the message you want to get across.

Don't Focus More on Visuals than Content

Snappy slides and whiz-bang graphics are all very well but what they do in most cases it takes the audience's interest away from the message and that just isn't anything to do with professional presenting. So remember it is content, content, content – made more interesting. Once you are finally satisfied with the message and how you want to say it then you can begin to think about a few slides to help the audience understand. A *few*! Remember, we are not trying to hypnotize them into getting the message. Advice? Keep it simple.

Just for Openers

Many presenters start off with a big slide on the screen. It usually has a BIG title and a BIG logo (and the date, in case the audience doesn't remember what day it is). This actually has the effect of making you look *small*, and it makes the audience look at the screen (waiting for something to happen) rather than at you.

Susan Says
If the screen is on the side and you are more in the middle of the room, more attention is naturally focused on you – and that is the way it should be.

Error number one, you haven't said a word and you've already lost most of them, because they are not looking at you.

For that reason, I like to start with a blank screen (more about blank screens later), that way there is nowhere else for the audience to look except at you. As I pointed out earlier, a lot of inexperienced or shy/nervous presenters use the screen as a way of diverting attention from themselves, that's the very last thing you really want to be doing when your role is to engage with the audience.

Having said that, if the audience sees your title slide as they are entering (a well-designed visual can often set a nice tone for what's to come) that's fine. But then blank the screen as you begin, so the eyes (and the ears too) are switched to you.

The slides are the message and you are hiding in the corner

You control the stage

You are the centre of attention – not the slides

Unless you have some exceptional reason, you should begin centre stage (no slides) and then step a little to the side when you are ready for your first slide. I generally go back to the centre when I blank the screen, only moving from that position each time you use PowerPoint and the audience needs to see the screen. This makes the whole presentation more intimate (even with a large group).

Talk to the audience without any visuals until you are ready for your first slide. That slide should come only when you feel it is necessary to make a point, not just because you are used to standing there with a visual on the screen.

When you do get started with the visuals, try for a logical build up. Don't make them the star of the show. Think always it is about you and engaging that audience.

The Bit in the Middle

As I said in Chapter Four, you can start and you can finish, but the bit in the middle is the meat in the sandwich. The examples and evidence you use in the message of your presentation are usually good places to use slides. Your visuals can carry the story, enhancing it, making the audience want to know more – more than you are telling them. And the way to do that is keep it simple and direct. The easier the message is on the ears and the eyes the better the audience will understand and accept it.

Too many slides

The fastest way to lose an audience is to have too many slides. Over the years, ever since PowerPoint and its cousins have taken over, we have been in the midst of slide creep. These days, it is quite common to see a 20 minute presentation feature 30 or even 40 slides. That's one slide every 30 seconds. Now who can keep up with that – not even the presenter?

Susan Says

If you follow my suggestion of building the presentation structure FIRST and then deciding where slides would enhance the message second, you should be on track for having the right amount of visuals.

Think it through. Write down all the messages then start to edit them down to a manageable number. My thought for a 20 minute session is between eight and 12. Sure that can be hard to achieve, simplicity – and therefore clarity – usually is.

PowerPoint experts advise that you take the number of minutes you have been given to speak, divide by 2, and that should equal about the number of slides that would be appropriate for that time slot. For example, a 20 minute presentation should have no more than 10 slides (or say 8 to 12 to give you some flexibility). You may need more (or less), but if you are way over that guideline number, take a good, long look at your slides and see where you can cut something out. Go back to your original paper-based presentation outline and see if some of the visuals are really necessary.

Too much information – or TMI, TMI

The next great sin is packing too much information onto each slide. Everyone does this. Engineers have build-up slides that look like grandma's spaghetti dinner by the time they are finished; marketing vice-presidents love colour overlays and charts that are a meaningless swirl of confusing designs. And they're surprised when the shareholders revolt. That "keep it simple" advice extends beyond the number of slides to the amount of stuff (electronic goo) you put on each.

Philip Brun, an executive with ST Microelectronics who listens to numerous presentations made to senior management, says that most people do not know the difference between data and information. Senior managers don't want data – they want you to give them information.

The six by six rule – when you have to use words

Many long-serving presentation professionals swear by the six by six rule: no more than six lines of text and no more than six words on each line. If you can edit down to that you're on your way and the audience is well on their way to comprehending what you're talking about too.

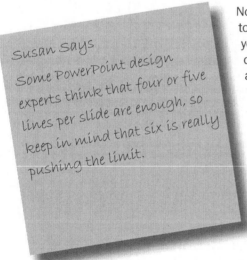

Susan says

Some PowerPoint design experts think that four or five lines per slide are enough, so keep in mind that six is really pushing the limit.

Not that limiting the number or words and lines is easy to do, but it can be done and it really concentrates your mind on what's important and what really doesn't have to be there. Think of it, just six lines and just six words. Real bullet points. Use only key words, not complete sentences or phrases in bullets and go easy on the adjectives as well.

Why they call them bullet points

Bullet points are so-called for a good reason, they are supposed to make an impact. A 20 word bullet point is a pop-gun and wouldn't impact on anything. Of course cynics say that they are called bullet points because that's what the audience would like to fire at you when you bore them!

Another point to keep in mind is that if your slides are going to be used as handouts as well as projected, put the complete details into "Speakers Notes," so that the actual slides on the screen are the cleaner – edited – version and the audience can read later the more detailed part in the handouts. Do remember to change the notes when you redo the presentation for another audience. I know one speaker who left the notes he had developed for a competitor when he gave his handouts to another client – not a good experience!

Susan Says

One exception on slides. If you're forced to supply material that is really too small to see on the screen (financial information is sometimes miniscule) then always provide the audience with a hard copy so they can follow what's going on.

You're just my type

Make sure that you pick a nice clear typeface for your words. Don't try and be clever, the thing is for the audience to read it. So make it big, bold and free of fancy curlicues. This is not the place for Romanesque lettering. A sans serif typeface is best of all (see box). Arial (bold when possible) will do just fine. If you use a serif font (such as Times Roman) put it in the slide title, not in the body. Try not to use anything smaller than 24 point, which you won't if you stick to the six-by-six rule.

Serif or Sans-Serif?

A "serif" is the fiddly bit at the ends of letters in some fonts, eg:

Times

Fonts that have them are called "serif" fonts and those without are called "sans-serif", eg:

Arial

The serif has one interesting side effect – it slows your eye down as you read.

As a result, when you read a block of text in a serif font it will take you longer, but because of that you will find it easier to understand detailed information. With a san-serif font you will get the message faster. For that reason, many newspapers use san-serif fonts for headlines (quick impact) and a serif font for the story (getting the detail). So, now you know why Arial is a better font for bullet points – quick impact, get the message and now focus back on the presenter!

Bring on the pictures

If you have seen the Oscar winning movie *An Inconvenient Truth*, you would know how visuals were used throughout the length of the production. The entire documentary is really just former US Vice President Al Gore making a presentation using visuals. But, do you see many words on the screen? No! It's doubtful Gore and his team would have won so many awards for the film if he had stood there with a bunch of bullet points appearing on the screen. The pictures of climate change have much more impact than words – a point to keep in mind during your planning process.

> *Susan says*
> Organizational charts without pictures are pretty boring. I am always amazed to see HR presentations about people where there are <u>no people</u> in the slides, only words and numbers.
> Pictures of your team, employees, customers make excellent additions to visuals.

Where possible, get rid of the text and use pictures and graphics that make your point. That much-used phrase, "a picture is worth a thousand words" was never truer. I have conducted dozens of studies where I asked the audience what they remembered from the slides they saw and 99% of their recollections were the pictures!

If you're looking to your team to meet certain objectives, make those objectives clear. But try to add a picture of the team in there somewhere, it does everyone good. Similarly, if you quote experts, use the picture of the person you quote if you possibly can. Pause in your delivery to give the audience a moment to read the quotation, then you read the words aloud.

If you speak about one of your manufacturing plants or other facilities for example, a photo makes it all a lot more real. The list for this goes on and on, but the rule here is: wherever possible, get rid of the words and use images (even corporate names can be turned into pictures of company logos).

And don't forget that statistics are data – charts provide information. What does your audience want from you? Information. The slide below represents a very simple way to convert data to information using a chart. The illustrations below, show the "visual" difference between data and information. Now which would you rather try and get your head around?

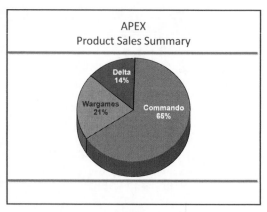

APEX Product Sales Summary	
• **Delta Video Games**	**14%**
• **Wargames Simulator**	**21%**
• **Commando Video Games**	**65%**

Here are more slide makeovers that demonstrate how pictures and simplicity work together to give better information and create more interest.

Perseverance

"In the confrontation between the stream and the rock, the stream always wins, not through strength but by perseverance."

H. Jackson Brown

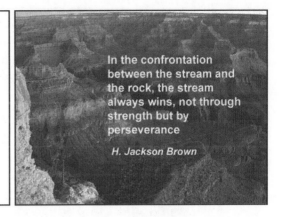

The quotation is more interesting with the picture of the Grand Canyon.

Required Actions

- Reduce office cost overhead
- Improve accounts receivable time frame
- Increase cash flow
- Reduce overtime
- Centralize all purchasing functions
- Reduce billing costs
- Develop strategic plan with field
- Reduce technology delivery delays

Challenges

- Improve profitability

- Reduce down time

- Centralize admin

- Plan strategically

Here the message of actions is stronger when you show the people who will make it happen. Don't put all the bullets on the same slide – you may need other slides to elaborate key ideas.

Project Goals

- **To investigate the ICT global template by reviewing its current functionality and identify improvement areas**
  1. Task began with a general review of the theoretical aspects of enterprise resource planning (ERP) systems
  2. Interviews with persons familiar with the functionality and experience in use of ICT or other ERP systems occurred
  3. Other companies' experiences with ICT and their use of additional functionality to gain greater benefit from the system was reviewed

- **Give recommendations for further enhancement of the potential benefits of ICT within our company**

Project Goals

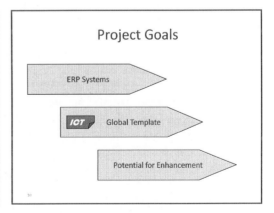

Why use all of these bullets when a few key words are all the audience will comprehend. The speaker should fill in the details verbally. If the audience needs the details for later, put them into "Speaker Notes" in PowerPoint. But don't make the audience read all of those words!

Black slides and the "B" key

I've never understood why presenters – even some of the better ones – see the need to keep the large screen illuminated and the audience's attention away from them throughout the whole delivery (remember what I said about the opening earlier?). What I like to do is drop in a "black" slide that effectively turns off the screen. This gets the audience's attention straight back to you, if only because there is nothing else to look at. Try it. It really works. And by the way on most keyboards in presentation mode, depressing the "B" or the "." key has almost the same effect.

Making it Clear as Black and White

A black slide is where you use the rectangular drawing tool in PowerPoint to draw over an empty slide and then fill it with black. I make one and then paste it into the presentation whenever I want the audience to look at me, not the screen. Dropping in black slides also helps me pace myself and my message. Using the "B," or the remote mouse blank function works as well too. The only difference is that instead of moving later to your next slide, you will first go back to the old slide. Remember, using the black slide keeps you moving forward all the time.

If you are not clicking through your slides quickly, remember to set your computer so that your "screen saver" does not go on when you have not touched your mouse for some time.

Slide Rules

If you're showing slides, it's a good idea to make sure that the audience can see what's on them – that, of course, is what they are there for. If you've followed my advice and kept the words on a slide to a minimum you shouldn't have too much of a problem, but remember where you are going to be presenting. If it is a big auditorium will the audience at the back be able to read those words and see those pictures? I try never to dim the lights in the audience (disaster for the after lunch bunch), but minimize any lights directly around the screen for better visibility.

Susan Says

If you get the chance of a rehearsal onsite, make sure you go to the back of the room to know if you can see your own slides clearly. And check to make sure you don't block your audience's ability to see the screen when you move around.

Colours and contrasts

A lot of any audiences' ability to make sense of your slides will be the colours and the contrasts you choose. Clearly, the best contrast you will have will be black on white. Many companies that have used the dark background and bright white text have realized that it did not work so well in large rooms or auditoriums. So lighter background and dark text are used more and more. I never cease to wonder at how many people use a dark blue background and then black font. About the only colours that work with dark layouts are white and yellow – shadings tend to diminish readability even more.

I prefer a light background with a black font and I use colour in titles, lines, and bullets. The simpler the better. Again this is all about common sense and trying it out before you subject an audience to struggling to make out what you have put up on the screen. Nothing – even you being boring – is quite the turn-off of not being able to read something. Eventually audiences just switch off completely and you have lost them. So, just like getting a friend to listen to you, get a friend to look at your presentation too. It will pay off and I guarantee you will change something.

Most companies have corporate templates for slides and other graphics that have to be used in presentations. Some of these are better than others, but your communication department has devoted a lot of time and effort to making slides graphically consistent, so find out what your organization standards are and use them. More about this later.

Animations, flying titles and other distractions

Remember when we first started using PowerPoint and people discovered all of the possible animations and other wonderful whizz-bangs that were available?

Some of the worst presentations I have ever witnessed had every bell and whistle that could be found. Titles zoomed in from left and right, with swooshing sounds to emphasize their arrival (some, I recall, favoured the staccato of a machine-gun). Video clips (with poor graphics) further stirred up this creative mess. No one was paying any attention to the message; they were steeling themselves for the next primeval scream from the screen. This is not – and never will be – the way to get an audience's attention. If they want these sorts of graphics they'll pay money to go to a horror movie.

This was once beautifully summed up by the chairman of a conference where it seemed everyone had animated presentations, videos and film-clips. Frustrated perhaps by the lack of real human contact with the audience he announced. "Next year, we won't ask you to go to the trouble of coming here, we'll just mail you the DVD." Hopefully at least some of the so-called presenters got the message.

Discreet animation is OK. If you want the audience to see only one bullet point, chart, etc, at a time (and you usually do since they will look ahead if you do not), animate these discreetly and you control what the audience sees and when you want them to see it. If you are discussing the first bullet on your slide and the audience is already trying to read bullet five, you are not communicating! But any animations should be gentle ones, like a "wipe" from the left or the top of the page. *Never flying bullets* – please.

I also like gentle slide transitions so that going from one slide to the next is not so abrupt. "Wipe right" or "uncover right" are simple options that allow you to move from slide to slide with easy, flowing motions.

If you print your slides as handouts (six or nine per page) and number each slide, you can go to any slide immediately by entering the slide number and pressing the either "Enter" or "Return" key on your computer. That means you can take a question and go to the correct explanatory slide without going through all of the animations. For example, if I know the information I need is on slide 12, I would type 12 and "Enter."

Susan Says

One of the best investments I've made is a remote mouse. I use a very simple one (Interlink Navigator) that lets me stand anywhere and change slides, go back, go forward, blank the screen and use animations. There are only four buttons on the device (so you can't get confused) and it fits comfortably in your hand.

Pointers, lasers and confusion!

It's not just flying titles that drive people crazy. Someone, somewhere, sometime invented the laser pointer. You couldn't manage to distract an audience more if Darth Vader had appeared with his light sabre. Just watch an audience, they don't look at you, they don't look at the slides, they don't look at the words, they look where the little red dot of laser pointer is going to go next. If you want to mesmerize an audience this is the way to go and I can guarantee they will leave your session remembering *nothing*.

Susan Says

My remote mouse has a laser pointer that I <u>only</u> use when someone has asked a question that requires my "pointing" to something on the screen. I do so carefully and slowly. Otherwise, I prepare circles or squares to identify items on the screen I want the audience to see - animated when I want the audience to see them.

The left chart compares a great deal of information that the audience would see at the same time. While the viewers need to compare all of this data, they will have a difficult time focusing on the part you consider important. Using a laser pointer to indicate the significant bars is not as effective as building and animating a circle around the selected items, as shown on the right.

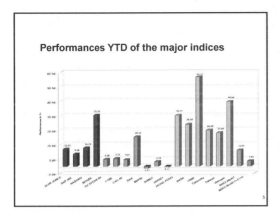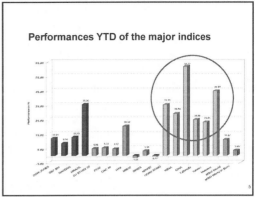

The circle should be animated. By presenting the chart and then bringing in an animated circle around the key figures you can concentrate your audience's attention.

Funny film clips

I know they are so tempting. Put in an amusing film clip and watch the audience convulse with…? Well I'm not sure what, but it won't necessarily be praise. Unless it's the CEO's retirement party, leave out the jokes and the movies. I know a sales director who put up a movie of his dog doing tricks – there was supposed to be a link in there somewhere. We are all still looking for it. Meanwhile he's in a corporate sales territory that makes a Russian gulag look like a spa resort. So, no funny material (unless you are sure it will work) – please.

Having warned you off the idea, there are moments when a quick dip into the humour box can pay off. The word *quick* is the one to concentrate on. Training sessions can be greatly improved with some good clips that add humour and interest to the sessions. Funny or amusing pictures can also entertain and enlighten. I have seen speakers bring photos from their holidays or favourite sports or hobbies that made a more serious point and added a great deal of interest. All of these creative additions worked because the speaker added value with the pictures and clips, as well as interest.

Endings

If you haven't followed my advice, the ending probably doesn't matter, because by that time no one will be conscious enough to care. But if you have made it through your allotted time with a nice, easy-to-follow, uplifting message then you have to do three things:

- summarize and tell the audience what they should do next
- take any final questions
- close smartly, leave them wanting more

Don't leave with lingering images on the screen. Leave them with just you on the stage. That's what this has all been about hasn't it: you and the audience.

My advice is turn off the projector for your closing (your summary of next steps may be on a slide). Some people insist on leaving their name, logo and website on the screen. Who cares? Certainly not the audience already scrambling for the exit to be first in line for the buffet lunch. You can give them your contact information as a handout after you speak. Make sure they are left with the final image of you, the person who just delivered that very professional, direct, to-the-point speech. The one that really hit your SOCO right on the head.

Now let me backtrack for a moment and fill you in on some other things that might be boring at first look, but are important.

Corporate rules on design

Susan says
If your corporate template includes an unusual font, check to see that your visuals downloaded properly. Unique fonts are not loaded on all computers and using them may result in some blank or distorted slides - another reason why it is important to rehearse on site, using the equipment that is available for the real presentation.

Most corporations have a style book and template that details just how, where, why and when you can use the logo or brand. This is important, so get a copy and use it. Do not try to be clever here and reinvent the brand, change the design, colour or anything else about the product or service – people have been fired for less and you do not want to tempt the corporate sprites who are guardians of the brand – 'cos believe me they are out there and they can be very, very tenacious

Permissions and copyrights

If you are using other people's materials or ideas you may need to tell them. Most of the time if it is a simple quote or the mention of a product you are OK, but do be careful. Some companies thrive on suing people (it's built into their corporate DNA). Message here, if in doubt, check it out. And consider carefully that pictures can be dangerous, music even more so and a clip from major film or TV show even worse. There are lots of websites where you can obtain pictures that are free of copyright or at very little cost. Microsoft has numerous images online that you can use with PowerPoint. Your own organization probably has many you can use. Consider using pictures you have taken yourself as well.

But being sensible here, playing a (short) blast from the past or an (equally short) rave from the grave is normally OK. The context of your presentation is relevant as well – what you can get away with in a small internal presentation to members of your team is one thing, what you can get away with in public presentation that you are benefiting from commercially is quite another. Like I say, if in doubt, please check it out.

Travelling with visuals

The best advice here is to send (by email unless the file is too large) a copy of all your visuals in advance. That way the organizers have them and will normally have their technical people load them up ready. Some people I know insist on using their own equipment wherever possible as they feel more in control.

Whatever you decide to do, there is one very important point here. Check out that your presentation has been loaded properly, that every image is there. Computers are logical, the people who work with them aren't!

Additionally, I always have my presentation on a memory stick that can easily slip into a pocket. This gives you instant back-up in case something goes wrong. It's also handy to have a few spares around – very useful if a prospect or a senior manager wants a copy at short notice.

> **Susan Says**
> Never forget to check that your presentation has been loaded correctly by the technical staff well before your slot on the program. How many times have you seen the speaker say "Ah, that is the older version of my slide show"? Check, check, check.

No copies in advance

One thing to watch out for if you send copies in advance, make it a condition that your slides are not replicated and given out to participants before hand. I've said this before, and I'll stress it again, advance materials are just another distraction. If you want to stand on a platform and look at the tops of people's heads as they follow your screen slides in their notebooks fine – but they should be looking at you. Nothing wrong with hand-outs AFTER you've spoken, but not before. And, yes, I know, some audiences will demand advance copies, and you may not have much choice. But if you can choose, give out your "leave-behinds" following your presentation.

> **Susan Says**
> Do be careful that the audience can still see the screen when you move. Check it out.

Freedom to roam

If you are using a remote mouse you're free to move around. Pacing is not a good idea, but some movement when you change a point, for example, can reinforce your messages.

Don't forget

The key to a good presentation is *you*. So, don't reach for that PowerPoint button until you know what it is you want to achieve. And if you can do it without visuals (and without notes too), you'll get a lot of attention. I just bet some of your audience would never have seen anything like it before. One thing, they'll remember you and your message long after the guy with 50 slides is but a mere blur in their memory.

Propping Up Your Argument

How effective would Steve Jobs, Apple's CEO, have been when he introduced the new iPhone (slowly taken from his pocket), or the MacBook Air computer, (little by little appearing from an interoffice mailing envelope), if he had shown them on a screen. Not nearly as dramatic as the "real life" effect. This technique is called using "props," short for the word "property" which is a theatrical term to indicate items that actors use on stage. These are real, three dimensional objects that are also visuals – but visuals that you can hold.

Just like using PowerPoint or other visuals, props are there for one thing only, to enhance the message or possibly make it more exciting. Long-standing professional speakers usually have some of their favourites, tried and tested over many years. What looks easy for them, may be difficult to pull off for the novice presenter. You have to practice over and over with them to make sure the "demonstration" works faultlessly – every time.

Therefore, as with visuals, keep it simple until you have the confidence to do something out of the ordinary.

Here are some thoughts on the use of props.

I recommended a CEO use a Rubik's cube (that infernally complicated cube game) to show how hard putting together a new organization was after a recent takeover (the story was that, "he wouldn't be able to answer many questions at that time due to the complexity of the new business").

Use the product that you are trying to sell (even better to take this one step forward and let the audience use it too). That means giving them time to do an exercise of some kind. Advice: don't try to continue talking while the audience is passing around the prop!

One top manager compared a current financial report to a simple, blank sheet of paper to show the team that they had an opportunity to improve results from the previous quarter by "delivering" the new results that would meet their goals.

People bring books, newspapers and magazines with articles and opinions they refer to as "evidence."

Others bring samples to give to the audience (usually better given out after the presentation). Audiences love gifts.

One of the more famous props is the "empty chair" that reminds the audience of the person the speaker is "debating" with.

When my brother-in-law, Plato Rhyne, retired as a Captain for Delta Airlines, he flew his last commercial trip and then spoke to a large group of company representatives, friends and family. It was a rather solemn occasion but he lightened the tone considerably when he said he had a few short comments to make and proceeded to unfold a long reel of the old fashioned computer roll paper that went on-and-on forever!

You can be creative and imaginative with props (like the Rubik's cube) or you can just bring the product you are talking about. Either way, your visual prop is something special and usually a lot more memorable than yet another PowerPoint slide.

The weird and the wacky

The smart people of this world have long known that props can support the grand gesture. And because they are part of the person (no one ever got famous with just a set of visuals except perhaps Al Gore), it means that the effect is so much greater. When French singer and songwriter Serge Gainsbourg burned a banknote on TV everyone talked about it. When then Soviet leader Nikita Khrushchev took off his shoe in the UN and banged it on the table it was world-wide news. Interestingly, the follow-up to that never made much impact but was equally clever. After Khrushchev put his shoe back on, the then British Prime Minister, Harold Macmillan, asked the interpreters, "can you translate that please? I didn't catch what he said." But it was the fiery Russian with the prop (a shoe) that everyone remembers decades later.

Now it is probably unwise to go to those extremes at the next management get-together, but the point is there. Grand gestures with props do make an impact. It is how you use them that matters.

One speaker I have heard about, Feargal Quinn – the CEO of a chain of supermarkets in Ireland who talked about the service ethic – was very short. Worried that the audience would take time to warm up to him he had a great way of getting their attention. He would arrive on the platform swinging an outsize golf club. He would then proceed to place a golf ball on the stage, and address the ball as if to hit it. Only one thing, the audience was directly in front of him. This got their undivided attention. Amazingly enough, this trick seemed to work even better in front of audiences who had little or no knowledge of the game of golf.

Finally, he took a mighty swipe at the ball, the audience ducked and the golf ball exploded! From that moment on they were wondering what would happen next.

Another speaker, Shay McConnon, in addition to being a top motivational presenter, is a magician. He uses magic in his act to focus people's attention onto him all the time; this includes the unlikely spectacle of half a gallon of water being poured out of a newspaper!

Now, none of the examples above may fit your style or your audience, but think out of the box a little to see if there are some props that might help you get your message across better. If they add value and interest, practise using them. The emphasis here is on the practising.

At Alstom, the giant French engineering firm, to mid-level sales managers created a fantastic presentation based on the game of rugby. One was French the other English, and they built the presentation based on the huge, age-old rivalry between France and England. Audiences loved it!

Also remember that props are three dimensional and they are with you, meaning the audience has to look at you. At their most effective, props actually bind the audience to you. So think long and hard how that can best be achieved. But the best way – always the best way – is to keep it simple.

Putting the product first

Product launches of course are a place where the speaker does come second. The star isn't you (shouldn't be you) but whatever you are trying to promote. Steve Jobs of Apple and Bill Gates of Microsoft are both great examples of people who have tirelessly and endlessly promoted their products on platforms around the world. Elsewhere the major auto manufacturers are renowned for their glitzy Hollywood style new product launches that have been adopted and adapted by the rest of the industry. This is certainly the one place where you are not supposed to be the centre of attention. That phrase "the car's the star" is, in this case, true.

> *Susan Says*
> *Presentation rules are there to be broken, as long as you know why you are doing it. But there needs to be a very, very good reason.*

I worked with a CEO recently who was opening a new chain of retail stores. Breaking the rules of the blank screen, we kept the new store logo on the screen in the background so that it could be seen continually – and hopefully remembered forever.

A word about security

One thing to keep in mind. We live in a security-obsessed age, so when you are travelling make sure that any of your props go in the checked luggage. Complex electronic items, joke items and so on don't just set off alarm bells they have the nasty habit of attracting official disapproval. Recently, a colleague of mine was stopped at an airport security check because he had a set of handcuffs (that he had used for years as props in a presentation) in his hand luggage.

That sort of hazard apart, props are what you make of them for yourself. They are there to enhance your presentation and keep that audience's attention on you. Remember, that's all they are there for.

Whiteboard and flip chart

You can't get more simple than a whiteboard or flip chart. These are the very basic props. But, like I said, just as visuals take the audiences eyes away from you, these basic props draw the audience to you. They also allow you to be more spontaneous if you feel confident enough to try it, because you can change instantly what you put onto them.

Often using a flip chart can make a presentation seem a lot more informal (which has its uses) or look a lot less stage managed. Remember, the very best presentations look effortless, they just take a long time to get that good!

> **Susan Says**
>
> Visuals can push people away from you, props make an audience look at you. But be sure to hold them to the side – not in front of you – so the audience can see them and you.

Also, whiteboards and flip-charts are great props if you want to involve your audience in your presentation. Many speakers use this technique to great effect, asking for audience comments and opinions. This can be a useful tactic if you want to break down barriers and it works especially well in small, informal groups.

I often work with speakers who have some artistic talent (sadly rarely used in their positions) and I really encourage them to use the flip chart and *draw*. Their talent can be very helpful in getting messages across. As I've said already, "a picture is worth a thousand words". It's also a lot more fun for the audience than static PowerPoint.

Edward De Bono, well known author and lecturer, keeps his audiences fascinated by speaking and drawing on an overhead projector. I once told him that I could never do that since I had no artistic talent, and he said "All the better. The simpler the drawing the better. If it is too good, it can be distracting." So whether you are an artist or not, simple, clear drawings can be very effective. If you write on the board, be sure to print carefully in large letters. Most of us use computers so much now that legible writing is hard to manage.

> **Susan Says**
>
> Tell them, show them, _involve_ them.

Bring your own pens because those on offer in meeting rooms (especially hotels) rarely work. I like Sanford's Mr. Sketch, scented pens. They last longer and have stronger colours. You may want to pre-draw some of the charts (they are usually more visually attractive that way) and add some lines, words, arrows as you talk.

Just as for PowerPoint, be sure to start with a blank page on the flip chart and then turn to another empty page when you are finished with the chart. Don't leave the old page on the chart if you don't want the audience to continue to look at it.

You can see how important the use of image are in helping to keep the audience focused on what we are saying and trying to get them to do. Visuals with lots of pictures and graphics, stories that build images in the mind, and props are key to audience attention and retention.

Now go try it for yourself!

Chapter 7

It's All in the Delivery

"The ability to speak is a short cut to distinction. It puts a man in the limelight, raises him head and shoulders above the crowd, and the man who can speak acceptably is usually given credit for an ability out of all proportion to what he really possesses."

Lowell Thomas: broadcaster and journalist

If you're in business, chances are you've already attended your fair share of presentations, seminars and conferences. And there's one thing I will bet, there are two or three speakers that you remember, not so much for what they said as how they said it. If you stop and think for a minute you'll realize that "how they said it" wasn't so much their voice, their phrasing or their delivery. It was about who they were. It was about how they made you feel when they said it.

In short, they were a presence.

Presence is extremely difficult – practically impossible – to define in pure objective, scientific terms. Some people just seem to have it. Others struggle forever frustrated to get it. It can't be defined by a person's physique or looks either. It's a special "something" that sets these people apart.

Whether you ever achieve that total, commanding presence or not, there are some basic considerations to take into account when you are on that platform. This chapter is going to help you recognize and utilize them. You may be surprised to find out that there are specific images we associate with creating that "presence", but once you know what those images are maybe, just maybe, you'll have that presence too.

It's Not What You Say, It's How You Say It

I'm sure you've heard that phrase, "hanging on every word." Well no one ever hung on a word, but what happened is that they were totally taken in by the presence of the person they were listening to. You see, it's really all about how you present yourself to an audience: how you say it, how you deliver it, that's what gets the audience's attention. And remember, it's their attention we are always trying to get. Because without that your message is stuck at the starting gate and going nowhere.

A Question of Authority / Stage Presence

Presence comes in a wide variety of shapes and sizes. Indeed over the years I have seen the most unlikely people transformed by the mere fact of stepping on a stage. You can almost hear the click of the switch as they turn on "the presence". And the stage doesn't have to be a big one either. Communication can happen just as easily one-on-one

Former US president Bill Clinton has "the presence" big time. Many people have told me that even if they were facing the other way, when he came into a room they felt something and turned around. And Clinton's ability is not confined to big groups, but being able to reach out to individuals in a crowd and make them feel they were the only person there.

Susan says
Presence, coupled with stagecraft, tied to empathy. All working together provides a powerful, unforgettable combination.

A colleague of mine, Hanneke Frese, described meeting Clinton at the Davos Symposium in 2007. "The room was packed with people, but when it came for my turn to meet with Clinton, I went up to him, shook him by the hand and he turned me around so that he was facing away from the crowd. He concentrated for my five minutes entirely on me – I WAS the only person in the room."

Interestingly, Jacqueline Kennedy Onassis was credited with this ability as well, and I wonder if the new first lady of France has it too?

Margaret Thatcher, the former British premier, had the "presence" too. Another colleague, Mike Johnson, a master speechwriter, went to a book signing in London in the late 1990s. "I got there early, and for some reason so did she," he recalls. "Her detective waited outside the door and there I was, alone, in the presence of this famous person. The room was set for an afternoon tea for 20 something people. Without breaking her rhythm, Mrs Thatcher walked over to the tea service, turned to me and said, 'shall I be mother, and pour you a cup?'. She was maternal almost, entirely at ease. This went on for about five minutes. Then the door opened and the rest of the guests came in. Instantly, she changed into this all powerful person. It was incredible, like Clark Kent going into the phone booth and coming out as Superman."

It would seem that "presence" can sleep at times but is always ready to reappear at a moment's notice.

But "presence" doesn't have to be overt in any way. Indeed it can be exactly the opposite – completely understated.

A great example of that is the late, great management writer and thinker Peter Drucker. Thousands of managers would flock to his lectures. What they got was an ill-kempt, short, professor. Not only that, he spoke with a strong accent, and never raised his voice. So what was the "presence" all about? In Drucker's case it was the words of wisdom, and how he told them. Wrapping up stories about management success and failure while delivering a history lesson. All of it delivered in a fairly monotonous, matter-of-fact tone. But he had presence. He also had charisma – that indefinable something that you could never quite put your finger on.

One of my colleagues spent time with Drucker in the 1990s, attending a series of lectures in Stockholm, Brussels, Paris and Vienna. "The most fascinating thing about Drucker was his pronouncements. You just knew he was right in what he said. You would write it down, take it back home and work on it. Imagine my surprise," he told me, "when I realized that many of the facts and figures he quoted as gospel in Stockholm, had all changed by the time we got to Brussels, changed again in Paris and were completely mixed up in Vienna!"

Yet, such was Drucker's "presence" that they were always the "right numbers" to whoever heard them.

Henry Kissinger, former US Secretary of State, is another low-key person, who speaks with a deep, accented monotone. But he comes across as incredibly intelligent with a very dry humour. I have seen his presentations many times and he held my attention the for the entire speech. People who met the diminutive Mother Theresa said she too had presence. Another, of course is Nelson Mandela. Again someone who never raises his voice.

It's All About Confidence

So what's the "presence" about and can you get it? To my mind the main key to achieving anything like "presence," or stage charisma if you like, is summed up in one word – confidence.

Everyone of those people mentioned above – Clinton, Thatcher, Drucker, Kissinger – had total confidence. Not just in themselves but in their message. They were believers. They may have been wrong about a thing or two, but they believed in what they were doing and – consequently – in who they were. There was never any self-doubt, or if there was it didn't show.

Having that level of confidence in who you are and what you stand for gives you the unique ability to deliver the same message day in and day out without it ever sounding tired or lacking in enthusiasm.

Susan Says
Confidence and self-belief can carry you a long way - but you need to know your stuff too, just like the Clintons and Thatchers of this world.

Susan Says
I work with many top managers who feel confident in most aspects of their jobs - until it comes to speaking in public. Then the confidence wavers. So part of "presence" is knowing how to look confident - even when you do not feel confident.

Pitching Your Personality

If you have the confidence and you believe in the message, I think you are half way there. But the belief must be there too. There's an old saying that "you can't get a salesman to sell something he doesn't believe in." I'm sure that's true. Great salespeople can't sell bad products, not for very long anyway.

The same goes for you on that platform, addressing that audience. You need to feel that you are communicating something that they *need* to hear. You must believe in your product, service, plan, revolution, or whatever it is you have chosen to sell to others. Perhaps, even more important, you need to believe in yourself.

Whether it is Bill Clinton, Margaret Thatcher or Joe down at the used car lot, they all believe and passionately want you to believe too.

Susan Says

Let's be realistic here. Sometimes your commitment to your topic is not as strong as you would like. If you are delivering information you are not so comfortable with, your confidence will be challenged - therefore that presence on stage becomes more remote. One possibility when speaking about topics that we are less knowledgeable about, or even disagreeing with, is to begin and focus your presentation on the part you like the most. At least you get off to a good start that way!

So What Does Presence Look Like?

I promised that this chapter would help you identify the behaviours we associate with presence or charisma. But before we get to that, let's try out a short exercise.

What I want you to do is draw two pictures. On the left, draw someone you think is a Winner (a stick character is fine) and on the right put a Loser. It can be an athlete or a movie star, it doesn't matter. What's important is how you see the body language of a Winner and a Loser. Make sure your characters are full body – head to toe – with faces. The simpler the design here – the better.

Winner v loser

Winner	Loser

Now, look at what you've drawn. Do your pictures look somewhat like these?

What are the differences you see between your winners and losers? Start with the feet and work your way up to the facial expression. What is the body language of the "winner"?

Who takes up the most space? Probably the winner.

If you are like most people who draw these figures in my courses, you will see the winner tends to:

● be more balanced, with better posture

● have the hands at the waist level and more away from the body – more open

● has a more animated facial expression

● looks directly at you

Perhaps your drawings are different, but I've had both individuals and teams from all over the world (Tokyo to Geneva to New York) do this exercise and no matter what culture they represent, the pictures usually look just the way I described above. Even in Japan, where direct eye contact is not used as much as in Western culture, the Japanese teams usually drew the eye contact part too. Additionally, body language for the winner tends to be up and open with movements toward the audience.

The eyes are the windows to the soul

I once saw the French singer Charles Aznavour perform to a crowd of over 1,000 people. The spotlights were on him, so he could see very little of the audience, yet he seemed to see every single person there. He knew where the seats were and made sure that, despite the bright lights, he "looked" at as many people as possible. He is a consummate professional who understands the importance of drawing in the audience by "touching" them with his eyes.

The "Silent" Language

But let's leave the eyes and move to the "silent" language of presentation. What do you do with that body of yours?

Balance

The first thing you need, and not many people ever think about this at all, is balance. Your feet should be aligned with your shoulders, knees flexed, weight equally distributed on both legs (if you play golf, this should be easy). If you move (not so good in the very beginning of your presentation), only do it with some purpose in mind – no pacing. Moving when you make a new point in your presentation can emphasise the statement. Conversely, moving in the middle of an explanation can dilute or weaken the meaning.

Gestures

Keep your hands above or at the level of the waist. If your hands start in that position, your body's energy will usually allow them to gesture in a natural way. Hands and fingers should have strength in the gesture. Be mindful of keeping wrist movement straight (not bent) that should strengthen gestures. Be careful too of keeping the elbows too close to the body.

> **Susan Says**
>
> If you begin with your hands by your sides or lower than the waist, you look (unfortunately!) like a penguin when you gesture.

Many men (not too many women) like to keep a hand in a pocket (probably a nervous reaction). Try not to start that way and don't keep the hand there too long (make sure there are no coins that are being jingled in there). Never put both hands in the pockets or you will look very small indeed. Interestingly, very nervous presenters almost always push both of their hands deep into their pockets (a way to make us small enough to almost disappear...).

Remember too that gestures can be much broader when you have a large space. But, conversely, if you are on television (or some closed circuit TV), keep your gestures very close to your body. TV magnifies everything and even the smallest movements look huge on camera.

Posture

There's not all that much to say here except, "yes", your mother had it right. Stand up straight! Look proud to be there. Funny how good posture also makes us *feel* better.

Making eye contact

If you see a child who has something they don't want to tell you, be sure they will look away from you when they speak. Good eye contact (in Western audiences at least) means sincerity and honesty. Look at as many people as possible for an instant (two to four seconds). If you have a large audience you can look at each section and everyone in the vicinity will feel you looked directly at them. If someone asks a question, respond by looking at the questioner, then "invite in" the rest of the audience with your eye contact. Fifty percent of your eye contact goes to the questioner and the other fifty percent should go to the audience.

Put on a happy face

The winner picture I asked you to draw earlier probably showed the character smiling. Most do. And that's the face you want to project to your audience as well.

OK, if you are giving your audience bad news you may not want to smile while you do it. But you might still approach the audience with a friendly face and then become more serious as you get to the "not so good" parts of your speech. Facial animation (happy, sad, serious, concerned – even angry) should reflect the content of the message. If the face says something different than the words (a grumpy face telling the audience how happy the speaker is to see them), you will trust the face over the words every time.

Lessons from the Lectern

A word or two about your lectern is appropriate here too. It isn't a castle, or a wall or a magic shield to hide behind. It is useful for holding notes (if you have any) and water. Apart from that, it gets in the way.

Look at the two samples below. On the left, the speaker is somewhat hiding behind the lectern, while on the right, the speaker has firm control of the stand and has put her energy over it – presenting a more commanding presence.

Some years ago, I coached a new CEO who felt at a great disadvantage because he was following a company leader who was an outstanding speaker. The new CEO felt competent in the job – but had no confidence as a speaker. It turned out that the big problem for his confidence – and his image – was that his predecessor was a much taller man. I quickly realized that the issue wasn't the difference in height but that the lectern in the company auditorium was made for a much bigger person.

But the solution was wonderful. Instead of building a new, smaller lectern that he would fit comfortably behind, the new CEO went one better, he just got rid of the lectern. The ghost of his predecessor was quickly banished!

And getting rid of the lectern is good in many ways. If you have to use one, get the size right and keep your hands up high on the sides, but you'll seem much more open and sincere by moving away from it completely. If you have a microphone that allows you to be mobile, take the opportunity to depart from the more formal stand and get closer, on many levels, to your audience.

Susan Says

I was arranging my notes on a lectern for a speech to the Geneva Press Club. The young man who was hosting me asked, "Oh, do you speak from the lectern? We usually speak from the heart." Needless to say, I left the lectern completely alone that day!

What Does Presence Sound Like?

You can probably get away with poor posture and "hiding" behind the lectern. You cannot get way with a poor voice. This means that you have to deliver in a voice that commands attention. Depending on how much speaking you are planning on doing, if you don't have much in the way of a strong voice, getting a voice coach might be a useful step that will pay dividends in the long run. So let's hear a few things about voices.

Can you hear me?

Let's start with the volume. Can you be heard? If not, consider working with a voice coach or using a microphone (or both). Practising being heard by everyone in the room is very important – even in meetings you attend (some of us forget this very obvious, day-to-day situation).

Enunciation or articulation

Native speakers of any language can become sloppy in pronunciation. Mumbling is not a good idea when people understand your language well, so you can imagine how difficult it makes comprehension for an audience whose level of the language is not very good. Open your mouth when you speak. Make sure all of the syllables are spoken clearly.

> **Susan says**
> Accents can be very attractive for a presenter. Your accent defines part of who and what you are so don't try and hide it. Just enunciate, articulate and use correct grammar and vocabulary.

This is even more important if you have an accent that differs from the perceived norm. Let me be perfectly clear: I don't think there is any such thing as an accent that is difficult to understand – but there are plenty of speakers who are difficult to understand. Many regional accents contract words, use non-standard grammar or local dialect words. If you have a regional accent don't try and change it – its part of who you are – just make sure that you speak clearly and people will understand you. The BBC is a great example of this. Years ago presenters and newsreaders all spoke with the same cut glass accent. Today you will hear accents from every corner of the country and the announcers are all perfectly understandable because they speak clearly.

Emphasize!

Even though people like Drucker and Kissinger as I've said earlier were successful with their monotones and heavy accents, you really want to use emphasis to keep audience attention. Emphasis includes stressing certain words, repeating words or phrases, changing volume, or.....pausing before or after something you say. When you pause, you'll create, in that short passage of time, something that every audience loves – anticipation. During rehearsals, learn to build in these pauses for emphasis and see how they change the tone of what you say. Record it, or better still film it and just see the difference it makes.

Pitching your voice

Susan Says
Learning to breathe very deeply helps at many levels. Your voice will be deeper, your pacing will be more measured, and for sure your stage fright will be reduced.

Audiences always seem to warm to deep, strong voices. Conversely the individual with a high reedy voice never gets the same attention. Margaret Thatcher trained her voice to be deeper – thus having more authority. The other thing to ensure is that the voice (your voice) that starts a presentation is the same one that ends the session. While that may sound silly, it really isn't. Try recording yourself and see how your voice changes pitch and tone during a 20 minute delivery. You may begin nervous (high) and then settle down. Later on (towards the end) there'll be a tendency to rush things and the voice can rise again.

Pitch at the ends of phrases and sentences

If you have ever heard someone who sounds as though they are preaching to the audience or speaking as though the audience was composed of children, they probably had a rising pitch at the end of most sentences or phrases. For instance, say the sentence, "It's nice to be here" in two different ways. First take the pitch on "here" *up*, and the second time take the pitch on that word *down*. Can you hear the difference? If the pitch goes up at the end of the sentence, you believe the speaker is asking if it's nice to be here, not saying that he or she is happy to be with you.

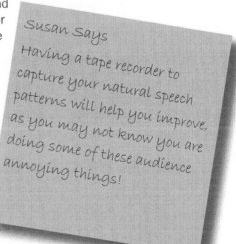

Susan Says
Having a tape recorder to capture your natural speech patterns will help you improve, as you may not know you are doing some of these audience annoying things!

We often speak to children in this way because it is not threatening. Each phrase sounds as though it is a question (or that you are not finished with the sentence). Some regional accents do this naturally – Swedish, Norwegian, Swiss German are good examples. But in English, hearing this repetitive rising pitch at the ends of sentences can be very annoying and tiring for the audience. Someone who has memorized material may end with this pitch as well – so be careful. Whatever the reason, try to vary the pitch so that it rises at the ends of phrases that are questions, or leading on to something else. Otherwise, be sure your phrase endings are definitive, using the down pitch.

Pacing yourself

If you watch really great presenters, you'll see just how well they pace their delivery. They never seem to rush. They are always in control, always making sure that the audience comes first by breaking those words up so you can hear each one.

> Susan says
> The speed of the voice is like the tempo of music. You should change speed to sound more interesting, moving faster (with good articulation) and then slowing down to emphasize key points.

The other thing all good speakers do is maintain that pace throughout their session. Amateur presenters often start off nervous and rush along (frequently because of shallow breathing). Later as they settle down they slow to a crawl. Try not to do that. During rehearsals have someone watch closely to make sure you keep up a nice steady, but varied, pace. As I've already stressed, try to have some agreed hand signals, so a colleague can help you speed up or slow down as necessary.

Maintaining pace and pitch is the sign of someone who's in control. Audiences like that, they feel comfortable. They are also less likely to be waiting to see what you, your voice or your body does next. If the audience is settled they can concentrate on listening to your message. One of Barack Obama's strengths is the quality and pacing of his voice. He understands the importance of the pause – and uses it.

Fillers – also known as animal sounds

Did you ever have a professor or a teacher who used so many "ums" and "uhs" in his lectures that you started counting them? An Irish negotiations expert that I know, Paul Meaney, calls these interruptions "animal sounds." Some people are so uncomfortable with silence that each pause calls for a "filler" – "ah", "uh", "er". A few of these are quite normal, but some people have way too many fillers, and the audience becomes distracted waiting for the next one.

Besides the sounds, there are phrases people use as well. "You know," "basically," "actually" are just a few of the words and phrases that pop out, that we should try and use less of.

These bad habits are hard to break and can increase, particularly when using a second language. This is where your friends and family can help. If you have fillers you would like to eliminate, tell colleagues you work with and your family to stop you whenever you use this sound, word, or phrase. You'd better warn them that the interruption will be very annoying, but it is the best way I have seen to break people of this bad habit.

Other phrases that can weaken our statements are "I think, I hope, or I would like." If I say "I hope this information was useful to you," I weaken the impact of the message. A phrase like, "I would like to show you today" is better emphasized by, "I will show you today." Small nuances in phrasing can either weaken or strengthen what we say. And note that this doesn't apply to just formal presentations. Being aware of how you say things helps in meetings and other day-to-day business activity as well. Never forget that "presentation" isn't always about a big deal speech.

Things better left unsaid

If there are words you have a hard time pronouncing, try to find another way of putting it, substituting difficult words whenever possible. You may be speaking a language that is not your first one, and most audiences are very sympathetic to spoken variations due to accents. But better to find an easier way to say it – remember it is all about communicating.

I worked with a doctor from a pharmaceutical company who kept mispronouncing the name of one of the company's products. Unfortunately, he had no choice but to use the word. After repeating the word 30 times, he was able to get it right. So if there are troubling expressions that you must pronounce, say them over and over until you feel more comfortable. Once more, it is all about rehearsal.

How to Dress

If ever the question, "what was the speaker wearing?" were asked to the audience after a presentation, the answer should be, "don't know exactly, but he/she looked very nice." What I am emphasizing here is that nothing you wear should be so distinguishable that it becomes a distinct memory. It should be appropriate and comfortable and leave it at that.

Find out what that audience is wearing and you can do the same (or perhaps a bit dressier or more formal). Do wear comfortable shoes – shined and in good condition. I recommend not wearing anything new (especially shoes) since you could have some surprises (labels that have not been removed, etc). The presenter usually feels a bit warmer than everyone else, so go for clothes of a lighter weight.

> *Susan Says*
>
> *If you are travelling, wear something you could present in - just in case the airline decides to send your bags on an unscheduled trip around the world. Most professional presenters have learned that the hard way (including myself).*

No sweat!

On the subject of being a bit warmer than your audience, watch out for colours! There was a huge media circus around a speech given by the then British prime minister, Tony Blair. Addressing a very hostile audience, he opted to appear in shirt and tie (no jacket). Unfortunately it was a warm auditorium and he was also pretty nervous – both causes for perspiration! He can't have been too pleased when the media showed endless shots of his light blue shirt, now noticeably darker due to the perspiration. Lesson: wear white shirts when you present without a jacket.

Need I say the outfit should be wrinkle resistant (one less thing to worry about) and check that there are no stains or spots (look at the back of your clothes before you put them on). And shirts should be laundered – home ironing is usually not the same for that 'finishing touch.'

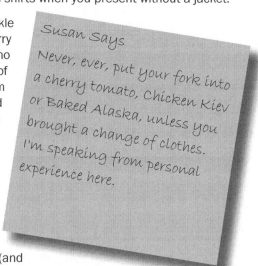

Susan Says

Never, ever, put your fork into a cherry tomato, Chicken Kiev or Baked Alaska, unless you brought a change of clothes. I'm speaking from personal experience here.

But even after the most careful preparation things can go wrong. A very nice man shook my hand quite vigorously while I was seated at a head table right before I made an after dinner speech. Somehow during this hand shaking, my arm (and jacket sleeve) soaked up a good bit of the dessert next to my plate. The whipped cream on my sleeve definitely was visible. When I began my presentation, I simply had to mention (with light humour) the reason for the spot on my cuff. Then I just continued. But if I hadn't acknowledged the stain, I would have been self-conscious the entire speech. I also learned my lesson about shaking hands close to filled glasses and fluffy desserts.

More tips for dressing for success

Other areas for distractions are clothes that are too tight, too bright or too revealing. Always remember that it is the message that is on show, not your wardrobe.

If you wear eyeglasses, make sure they have a non-reflective coating on them, so that lights bouncing off the lens do not hide your eye contact.

Additionally, earrings that dangle or large pieces of jewellery can be distracting – especially on television. The same is true for very dark nail varnish on women. Gesturing with brightly coloured nails can be distracting for an audience – not to say slightly scary too.

Always choose discreet, conservative clothing, unless you have a totally different agenda. But don't be so discreet that you blend with the background and cannot be seen. I understand that Margaret Thatcher's advance people would find out what colour her background would be so that she could wear something that coordinated well. Mind you, in her case, they just probably changed the background over night!

Mostly for women (not always), be sure your hair is pulled back so that your face is not hidden from the audience sitting on the sides.

If you sit on stage (with no table) think about skirt and sock lengths. Long socks for men who cross their legs are highly recommended! Although white shirts are good, white socks are the ultimate no-no. And empty your pockets!

My Pet Peeves

Over the years, I have listened to literally thousands and thousands of presentations. Sadly there are still some things that get on my nerves. More than that – and more of a problem – they get on the nerves of audiences as well.

To save your presentation and your reputation, here's a list of the things you *must not* do. Don't:

- pace during the presentation (moving with purpose occasionally can be good; pacing with no purpose is simply distracting)
- move from foot to foot – like a pendulum, you'll send the audience to sleep
- stand so that the audience cannot see the screen
- speak too quickly or too softly
- use lots of distracting fillers (ums and ahs to you)
- avoid looking at audience – especially looking at the slides more than the people in the room
- use the laser pointer as though you are in a Karaoke bar, underlining every word – the audience won't sing along (use the pointer sparingly – and then very slowly). Better to build in animations (circles that wipe around what you want to show) to highlight what you want the audience to see in your slides.

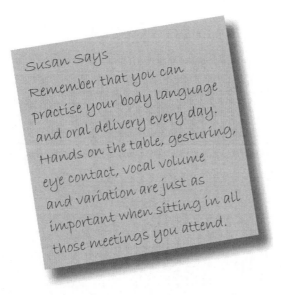

Susan says
Remember that you can practise your body language and oral delivery every day. Hands on the table, gesturing, eye contact, vocal volume and variation are just as important when sitting in all those meetings you attend.

Chapter 8

Dealing With Stage Fright

An amateur fears stage fright; a professional needs it.

Carroll O'Connor, actor

I turn pale at the onset of every speech and quake in every limb.

Cicero

He was one of ancient Rome's greatest orators but even Cicero had stage fright. I can feel for him. It's a feeling almost all of us get at one time or another.

I may have made thousands of presentations over the years, yet I sometimes dream that I am standing in front of a room full of people and realize that I don't know what I want to say. That is the ultimate nightmare for the presenter.

So far, I'm pleased to report that this has never actually happened to me, but the dream shows that even professionals have worries and an increased heartbeat when we present. We sometimes have a crisis of confidence too.

Like many of you, I am a perfectionist in what I do and I want everything to go perfectly. However, a perfectionist never feels entirely prepared. Clearly perfectionism is a mixed blessing so I have learned over the years to strive for excellence, not perfectionism. Excellence helps me set high goals for myself, but more achievable ones.

Sweaty Palms Time

But back to that inner monster, stage fright. Here are some good tips I have learned to deal with it and help others overcome it.

The first thing to do is identify the signs of the onset of stage fright:

- rapidly beating heart
- shaking hands (and legs too sometimes)
- shaking, uneven or high voice
- forgetting what you want to say (my nightmare)
- perspiration
- blushing

Do any of these (or all of them) sound familiar? If so you are like most speakers who find themselves quite nervous, especially just before and at the start of a presentation.

But why does this happen? Well, stage fright is probably both a learned and an innate fear. During our childhood, parents, teachers, even other children can make us very self conscious when we stand up in class, for instance. Because of that, we learn that people from whom we seek approval might not like what we have to say. Clearly, a child who is listened to at the dinner table grows up believing he has something to say more than the child who is tuned out or ignored. Parents beware of this!

Susan Says
Everyone gets stressed in one way or another. The trick is making that stress work for you, not against you. And keep in mind that the audience does not see what you are feeling. Most times, it feels much worse than it looks.

The innate fear we experience may come from the body's survival mechanism that goes into defensive mode when we "separate ourselves from the pack." All animals understand that they are safer when they are part of the group. When you separate yourself from the audience, there is probably a natural defence system that goes into play that says "Danger!" and the body starts producing hormones. Adrenaline is a big part of that cocktail of hormones and, among other things, it boosts the amount of oxygen and glucose to the muscles and the brain to help you to "fight or flee." Now you know why your hands and legs might shake and the reason perspiration breaks out on your brow. Yes! You're all ready to hightail it out of there, aren't you?

> Audrey Clegg, who I introduced earlier in the book (she is Director of Leadership Development for Wolseley, a UK firm that distributes plumbing and heating products) is a phenomenal speaker. She tells the story of the first time she made a presentation. It was a university recruitment speech and her boss was in the audience. As she began speaking, she froze, and simply walked off stage. Her boss, apparently a fast thinker, took the microphone and continued talking where she had left off. Audrey vowed at that moment to master the skill of speaking in public. She has not only mastered it, she is one of the most outstanding presenters I have ever seen.

One of best ways to calm yourself and have confidence is to do what Olympic champions do before a competition – positive visualization. Before your presentation, visualize yourself and your audience. Imagine that they are listening with interest, even visualize something going wrong and then see yourself fixing the problem without breaking your stride. The last part of this "movie" you create is when you see yourself closing and thinking, "I did an excellent job." Note, I did not say "I was perfect!"

That beating heart (blood pressure escalates), the lack of voice control (shallow breathing), and shaking limbs are your body's efforts to survive the perceived danger. In reality it is pouring extra energy in. Unfortunately it is doing this just as we want to appear cool, calm and collected.

But, all this extra energy can help us, if we learn how to use it correctly.

In the chart below, you can see how hypo-stress (very low stress) has a negative impact on performance (whether it is public speaking or playing a game of tennis or golf), while hyper-stress (very high stress) also has a negative effect. However, if you have a median level of stress, not extreme on either end, you get top or peak performance.

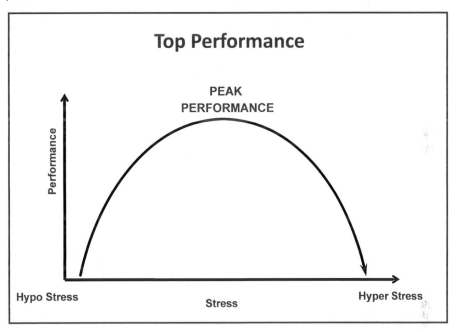

So, how do you get peak performance? First, by understanding why your body is going into this defence mode as the more you know what is happening, the less likely you are to panic when your heart starts revving up. Then again, another way to reach peak performance is to think about what kinds of events or people might drive your stress to the hyper-stress level, resulting in that diminished performance.

Think about presentations where you felt a great deal of stress. Why were you so tense and what happened? Working with speakers for so many years (and from suffering myself from some of these same symptoms) I have identified three major stress triggers:

- control
- conflict
- criticism

Control

Everyone dislikes losing control – and managers and senior executives like it less than most. If something doesn't go the way it should even the most well organized people can panic and go into hyper-stress, preventing themselves from being able to get back into control quickly.

Examples of the sudden loss of control in a presentation might be a computer crash, a shock or hostile question, a feeling of a lack of sufficient preparation (it won't be perfect!) or an audience not seeming to pay attention.

Tony Buzan, well known speaker, author and the originator of the Mind Mapping technique, says that we all need to lighten up when mistakes occur (because they *will* occur). His recipe when it happens? Just smile and say "fascinating!"

Conflict

When you bother to analyze it, conflict is a value. Think about it this way. If you grew up in a family where people sat around the dinner table and argued and debated every evening, you probably believe that conflict is a healthy and natural part of life. But if your family avoided conflict, or dealt with it in a negative way, you may suffer greatly when people begin arguing. Therefore, hyper-stress for you might arrive when you have verbally aggressive people in the audience or people who strongly disagree with your proposal. Conflict can help raise important issues in decision making, but people who find great stress in the conflict often cannot think of logical responses to those issues until much later. Not exactly ideal in the cut and thrust of a lively question and answer session! And this fear of conflict can block you from coming up with all the suitable responses you could have made to the verbal aggression if your brain had not been busy with emotional reactions.

Criticism

Much like conflict, how we see criticism has roots in how it first manifested itself for us as children. For example, if the criticism was constructive, we probably viewed it as a positive. But if criticism was negative, we can fear that kind of feedback and move to the hyper-stress area of performance when it happens in a presentation.

The worst part of these three Cs, control, conflict and criticism, is that the anticipation of them could result in a self-fulfilling prophecy – that we actually make things go wrong because we fear they will.

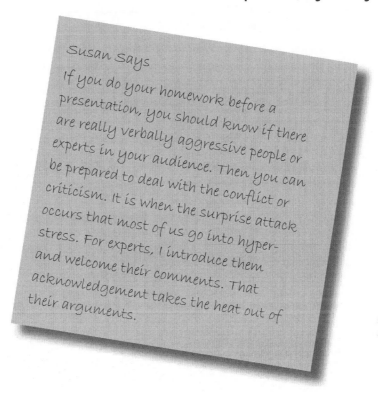

Susan Says

If you do your homework before a presentation, you should know if there are really verbally aggressive people or experts in your audience. Then you can be prepared to deal with the conflict or criticism. It is when the surprise attack occurs that most of us go into hyper-stress. For experts, I introduce them and welcome their comments. That acknowledgement takes the heat out of their arguments.

Go on – Just Lose It!

The key, I believe, is to anticipate the possibility that we may have to lose control sometimes and there is nothing at all we can do about it.

Yes, from time to time Murphy's Law is going to descend upon your presentation. Think of it this way – it happens. My advice? Give your audience a short coffee break while you fix the problem. In the great scheme of things, this is no big deal. That's, of course, unless you panic and the easy solution escapes you.

It all comes down to knowing when to control – when to be the very best – and when to let go, because that's the very best solution on offer. Whatever you do, don't lose it.

The same is true for handling conflict. Don't expect to have every answer (even though you did your homework well). It's OK to say "I don't know, but I'll be happy to find out for you." If someone in the audience has a different opinion from yours, it can make for a very interesting discussion or interaction. Indeed, some senior executives (usually the ones who have been through this type of "trial by fire") enjoy destabilizing junior members by asking provocative questions. Just answer the best you can, and whatever you do, don't take it personally and don't get angry. That will drive you into hyper-stress very, very fast.

Criticism can also be helpful if you extract the parts you believe will be useful to you. Some criticism might be well intended, but not necessarily beneficial. So put it aside as best you can, thanking the person who gave it to you anyway.

Some Other Techniques to Consider

Besides learning to manage control, conflict and criticism, there are other techniques I have used with great success for people who suffer from stage fright and first night nerves.

Susan Says
If your mouth gets dry, try the old actors' trick. Gently bite your tongue and the saliva will return.

Arrive where you are going to be speaking as early as you can so that you can check out your space and equipment and ensure that all is working well. Get comfortable with the site and all of the equipment. Remember, when you've checked it, check it again.

Make sure that you are totally "ready to roll" well before the audience arrives, that way you can "Meet and Greet" them. This has a very positive effect as you feel you will be talking to 'friends' instead of a group of complete strangers. Another way to calm those nerves is to arrive during a break or mealtime, so that you have time to talk with attendees. Rushing onto a stage with no prior contact with the audience is the hard way to do it. Be there early and give yourself all sorts of opportunities for interaction.

Even more than that, if you talk to the participants before you go on stage, you'll always find a few good stories. Referring to them and the people involved gives you an immediate rapport with the audience. And another thing: know your opening and closing cold. It's an old vaudeville trick – but it works. Even though you should have rehearsed everything, make sure you could do the start and finish in your sleep.

Susan Says
Balance your weight and don't move at the very beginning. Concentrate on centring all that extra energy!

Take a moment before you start to arrange your notes and calm down. Stop – Pause – look at your audience – Begin.

Try and remember to listen and link to other speakers, or members of the audience. I always try to link to something another speaker has said or an anecdote someone in the audience might have told me. This has an added bonus, because If you're so busy listening for something to link to, your mind will be occupied with what is happening in the room and that's much better than thinking about your stage fright. Also, you just sound more professional by linking what you are presenting to the comments of other speakers.

Breathe deeply, really deeply: deep breaths help lower your blood pressure, bring your voice tone down and help you pace your presentation. Honest, they do!

Don't take "their" easy way out

Another thing that can reduce stress is to politely insist on your own way of doing things. Don't be talked into cutting your presentation if it's going to lose its power or flavour, or message. Don't agree to run a discussion group if that's not the sort of thing you feel comfortable doing or if you think it is badly organized. Remember, presenting isn't just about what you do on the platform, it's about how comfortable you feel in any given situation. You want to feel good – make sure you give yourself every opportunity for that to happen.

Just give it your best shot

You don't want to be in a position to worry, so if the organisers don't make you feel comfortable there is one easy thing to do – don't go. Stay home and sell something instead. This is about you, this is about you giving it your best shot. And your best shot is as a well-rehearsed, confident presenter with a really good story to tell.

Your Notes Are Your Friends or Your Enemies

You may want to write down some of the key points or figures you need to use in the presentation. How you develop and use these notes can make a big difference in your performance.

First, use black ink if you hand write your notes (any other colour is hard to read from a distance), and write big block upper and lower case letters. If you use your computer to make notes, the Bookman Old Style (14 pt) font, double spaced will be easier to see. The letters should be big and bold. All capital letters are hard to read. We are used to looking at the word (like in newspapers, books and magazines) and reading the outline of the word, not the individual letters. So write the way you are used to reading.

I like large, white note cards. I use them vertically so that I don't write too much

Just key words. Number every page. I put my summary and closings on yellow cards since I may never look at the notes until I move to the summary and I can find the colour card easily.

When using notes, be sure to have two unread stacks in front (or to your side) at all times so you never have to turn your cards, but slide them instead. For instance, if you have five cards, card one is on the right and two through five are on the left. You can easily glance from card one to two without touching the papers. When you begin to use card two, slide it on top of card one, now you have pages two and three to see. Keep sliding until you finish the presentation.

Rehearse with those notes until you basically remember the placement of the word on the page. I underline the key phrases with black. However, most times I know what is on the cards so well that I don't need them at all.

Rehearse, Rehearse, Rehearse

That great hotelier, Conrad Hilton, built an empire of his three word mantra, location, location, location. Great presenters have their own phrase, rehearse, rehearse, rehearse and stage fright is reduced significantly with good rehearsing.

Watch and listen to a great presenter and the delivery looks effortless. In reality it is the result of countless hours of working hard at getting it just right. And by getting it just right, I mean knowing that it's so well developed that you *can* change it without any concerns.

If you know your speech backwards the wonderful thing is that you can easily change it, modify it and tailor it to individual audiences – quickly. You can also be in a better position to survive any meltdowns. That makes you an even better presenter.

One of my favourite phrases is attributed to Mark Twain and goes like this, "I wish I had more time to write you a shorter letter." Well the same thing applies to speaking. The more time you put in the tighter, sharper and more to the point it will be. What's more people appreciate professionalism. Slick sales patter apart, a truly tried and tested speech will always get attention.

So the rule is clear. Make sure you rehearse at every chance you get.

How to rehearse

People seem to rehearse best when they are in an environment that suits them. I know people who rehearse while shaving, jogging, cooking, driving. So a basic rule is, do what makes you feel good.

Others I know record their voice and play it back in the car. This is useful for getting ideas about emphasis and inflection and also allows you to listen to your voice and see where any problems are or opportunities are being missed.

Susan says
There's no single, best way to rehearse. Do whatever feels good to you. Just remember that rehearsing isn't the same thing as memorizing.

All the really good speakers I have worked with – and I've reinforced this in earlier chapters – have had the ability to create three or four great presentations (seldom more than that) and add to them as required by the audience. But they do rehearse them and continue to do so.

One of the greatest business-related speakers that ever was, Jim Hayes, president of the American Management Association in its heyday, had three speeches that shone like diamonds. But he worked on them all the time. So much so that in the course of about three to four years the whole speech would have evolved. Each year he changed something, updated another bit, added a better anecdote. That way, although the speech was essentially the same, it had an amazing freshness that always seemed to delight an audience, but he knew it because it was always so well rehearsed

Who to rehearse with

It always pays off to try out your presentation on someone. Of course the kind of reaction you get depends on who you pick. Your mother for example is probably not going to give you a truly honest opinion (well, she might), and neither are some of your co-workers or subordinates (some will be good at this and others will be too fearful of offending you). What you want is someone who can tell you where you may have gone wrong, the kind of things that are needed to tweak it into better shape and give a general opinion of where you are. Additionally, if this is some kind of a technical or professional presentation, someone who understands the content is vital too.

Possibly the best way to approach this is to develop a script (or outline), run through it a few times on your own and then get someone (or more than one) to sit and listen as you read it. Give them a copy as well so they can make notes as you go along. If you do this early in the process, you can have very good feedback that will help you prepare faster.

Once you've got the presentation more or less the way you like it, you can then set about learning as much of it as you can.

> Susan Says
> Don't forget to time the presentation when you've got it about the way you like it. If you know how long it is, you can adapt it to different situations and requirements. Try and rehearse it once or twice a day (or play a recording of it as you drive to work) and then go back to your helper and run through it again.

Even your enemies can help

This may not seem at all obvious as a way to rehearse, but I have a friend who thinks it really is the best way. We all have rivals in business, or wherever we're employed. Well my friend advocates asking them to help out. As he says, "if you want to get the hardest questions, ask someone who has a vested interest in seeing you not do too well." His view is that if you can get through a rival's close questioning you'll do fine when it comes to the real thing.

Can you over-rehearse?

Once you start dreaming about your presentation in your sleep, you've probably gone as far as you can reasonably go. However, I don't think you can really over-rehearse, just don't try to memorize the material. Unless you are so nervous that you can never really let go of this "chore" you have to get through, I don't imagine that keeping it at the front of your mind is very harmful. As I point out, all the best presenters are that way because of hours focused on getting it right. If it works for them then it will work for you too. The more you are thinking about your presentation, the more opportunities you spot for items to put into the speech (news stories, events, something someone says to you) – all of these make your final performance come alive, topical and to the point.

Rehearsing those "natural" movements

We've talked about body language and what it says earlier in the chapter, but it's important to remember than a lot of those so-called natural movements that top presenters make are the result of long hours of rehearsing them so they come out right every time.

That hand gesture, that head movement. They aren't necessarily just natural you know. Most successful people have rehearsed and rehearsed until they got them right – every time. Normally, if you feel confident with your material, and your hands start at the right level (see the earlier part on body language) your body's own energy will give you natural gestures.

True tales, or "why rehearsals pay off"

I've already referred to Javier Perez, the president of MasterCard, Europe. He is a very professional speaker, and he achieved this by quickly realizing that he had to work at it. He understood early in his career that, as a Spaniard, he needed help presenting in English. His dedication to rehearsal is a great example of what it takes to make a really professional speaker. He is also an example of the fact that doing it right from the outset pays off in your professional career.

Similarly, my story in Chapter Five of the Polish engineer illustrates exactly the kind of effort that's needed to make it work. Like most things in our professional lives, hard work does pay off. Unlike other things in our working lives, the ability to speak well in front of an audience can pay off in our private lives as well.

Another story illustrates why hours of rehearsal work. Alstom, the French high-speed train maker has lots and lots of engineers. Some years ago they were organizing a meeting for the senior managers and decided that one thing they wanted to do was to hear some views from the younger generation in the organization. Very much an engineer-dominated company – and very male-oriented too – they asked a young Spanish-speaking engineering graduate to come and present to the meeting. Not only young, this nervous 23 year-old was female!

Even more scary than appearing in front of a room full of senior managers, the presentation had to be in English! But professionalism took over from the outset and created a memorable moment. First a speechwriter was hired to help her develop the presentation. Then she rehearsed and rehearsed the session for three weeks before the big day. The result, she presented before an audience of 200 male engineers and spoke, in English without notes for 15 minutes. She received a standing ovation.

Afterwards she said it was the best experience of her life. Most interesting was that it wasn't just an experience she would remember, the audience remembered it too. But the result without the preparation would have been very, very different.

Just remember, in speaking in public, success is all down to those three words, rehearse, rehearse, rehearse. Well, not quite, hopefully the other things you have learned in this chapter will be useful too.

Chapter 9

Checking Out the Location

"Houston, we have a problem."

Apollo 13

"Remember Murphy's Law? Well, how about Sod's law: Murphy was an optimist!"

Anon

In Chapter Three I discussed the importance of the audience; how we all need to know as much about the participants to any type of presentations as we possibly can. Well the same goes for the location. Just as many presentations have been ruined by not knowing what the audience expects, so not being fully prepared for the meeting location has wrecked many a great presentation before it began.

There are countless war stories of where it all went wrong for even the most experienced presenter (some of them mentioned here) and most of them were based on not paying attention, not listening to the brief, making bad assumptions, or simply not asking the right kind of questions.

Anyone in business has had the same sort of horrible experiences. The meeting room where the sound, air-conditioning, lighting, power (you choose) doesn't work. The breakout room for 20 people that only has six chairs (or, almost as bad, having 20 chairs with six attendees – it looks as if no one showed up). The lectern control system with a mind of its own. There is probably no one in any profession or trade who hasn't suffered at the hands of inanimate objects. And the more technology we have access to, the more the problems are magnified. So today we have satellite links that don't link; microphones that won't switch on and then won't switch off; projectors inhabited by gremlins from another space-time continuum. All this apparently supervised by technical staff who live in basements and communicate in a series of inaudible grunts!

Having said that, most of us don't have lots of time to check out meeting venues that we are going to spend just a few hours in. For most of us the reality is, get to the venue, do your show and leave. However, there are times – key times in our careers – when we might want to spend a little more time on checking things out. The big event always demands your full attention. Get these opportunities wrong and it isn't good news.

So what I've done in the pages that follow is to work through a check-list that you can use for those big events. But you might want to do it as a matter of habit if you can find the time. As I keep repeating, the more we know about where we are going to present the better the delivery will be and the happier you'll make your audience.

Site Analysis

The term site analysis may seem like a rather grand title – certainly it is if you are just giving a talk at the village hall or your local tennis club – but it has its place, particularly where you are giving a major presentation that can have real career implications. Site analysis also is important if you get asked to organize events for others.

Site analysis is all about getting to grips with the whole of the location that has been chosen. Assuming that you don't have much control over that, you'll be surprised the kind of places you can end up in. Some of these can be quite bizarre (see box) and are usually based on organizers going for the uniqueness or quirkiness of the environment and letting that rule over practicality. Too often I have turned up at an event to discover that the CEO's secretary has picked some wonderful location: wonderful if you wanted to shoot a Hollywood movie that is, without any real thought of what effect it will have on people's presentations.

Fetch the gondola Luigi!

Organizers frequently get carried away by a location. One long-time colleague of mine arrived in Venice to address a conference of 200 people in a historic palazzo. Only problem was that it was the high tide season. The room he was to speak in began to flood at high tide and he addressed the group as they stood on the chairs! This doesn't help people to focus on your message.

Another friend journeyed to an alpine resort and woke up the morning of his presentation to a blizzard. Not only did half the audience never make it through the snow, the others spent the entire time gazing at the magical scene outside the window and frantically calling airlines to see if the planes were still flying.

The take away from this is, exotic locations look good in brochures and on Internet sites. For doing business they are very often horribly impractical.

OK, most of the time – if you're in business – you'll be in some fairly featureless auditorium, the kind of thing that every big hotel in every town in the world has on offer. But it isn't always that way. So whether it is you on the podium, your boss, or some visiting dignitary, you need to consider the complete layout of the venue and make sure it is appropriate.

By that I mean don't just look in front of you to where the audience is, look around you, down, up, to the sides and behind. It is behind you, the bit you don't see, but the audience does, that even tough old professionals forget about.

The background: what's behind you?

So intent are we on giving our presentation that we are apt to forget other considerations. After all you are there to deliver a message to an audience, isn't that it? Place looks OK, organizers know what they are doing, don't they? Well, in my experience, no they don't – not always at any rate. And that well-intentioned organizer is nowhere around when you are on stage battling a logistical nightmare. Remember, this presentation is your performance – no one else's.

For example, background can be a big issue. What's on the wall behind you; is there a view; will it cause a distraction from your message? I once carried out an outdoor site check for former President Jimmy Carter when he was speaking on urban renewal in San Francisco. Carter is known for abstaining from alcohol. As I walked the site to see what the cameras would be filming as he was talking, I realized that the main billboard behind him was advertising a bar! That just didn't seem appropriate for the president, so we modified the angle to show another view.

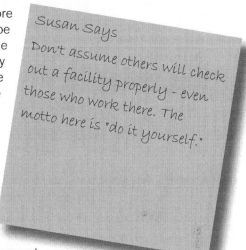

In London, I arrived the night before to look at the room where I would be speaking to a group of mostly male Middle Easterners the next day (see, I really walk the talk on these advance visits). As I stood at the back of the room, I saw what they would be looking at behind me – a lovely painting of scantily-clothed women. Now that was the last thing I wanted them to see as I lectured. So I asked the hotel's facilities person to remove the painting. He was not very enthusiastic (in fact, the artwork was tied into a security system and removal was not possible), but finally someone draped it. One of the workers chuckled as he was placing the cloth over the frame and said, "Prince Charles spoke in this room recently and made us cover the painting as well." I can imagine!

Susan Says

Don't assume others will check out a facility properly – even those who work there. The motto here is "do it yourself."

The background does not have to be so dramatic to be a problem. Too much light coming in the windows interferes with your slide contrast, a mirror behind you would be distracting, or any scene that might move or catch the audience's attention.

In these – and in so many other cases – the ability of the organizers to look around and see what's right before their eyes would have helped a lot. So remember, it isn't just what you see standing on the podium that counts, it's what the audience sees when it looks at you. And, most important, don't assume that others are going to be as aware of all this as you.

Impromptu Speeches and Interviews

The same goes for off-the-cuff speeches and presentations. Consider this. You've given your speech, the audience loved it. So much so that the local TV news channel want a few minutes of your time. Or even your own PR firm wants to capture a few moments for future use. They set up their pitch and you walk right into it. Again, look around you and specifically behind you! What is that camera going to record apart from your talking head? Over the years I've seen senior managers giving great speeches that just happened to have the logo of their largest competitor in the background. Others – not thinking – get talked into standing in crowd-filled corridors, in the middle of busy streets and with all sorts of activity going on behind them. If you want that message out – want to reach that audience – go back to my rule – stay in control. It is all about you. When you consider that today with so many images streaming from TV and the Internet, the chances of you not being filmed at some point are very slim indeed. In that case you need to be aware, be professional just like with everything else. Think about it this way: you prepare for a presentation, so prepare for these impromptu opportunities too.

Susan Says
For interviews, I suggest you reserve a one-on-one interview room at the site where you can control your space in anticipation of media requests.

Look Mom!... It's Me!

One of the worst background contrasts are media events where people who are part of the "background" shots have no idea they are on camera. So you have a company spokesperson giving a heartfelt serious briefing to the media, and a few people milling around behind who look like they are at a party, chatting and laughing. No one is invisible when they are on the "public stage," and it is good sense to realize that.

Susan Says
Don't be flattered by requests for interviews and agree to just any location. Check it out. Most important, what's behind you?

Most dangerous for distractions and surprises are outdoor events. I have seen many press conferences where low flying aircraft or passing traffic drowned out all possibility of hearing the speaker.

The Room

It can be a small meeting room, a conference room, an auditorium. That doesn't matter, the size is simply a question of scale. What does matter though is that for the time you occupy it, while you are on that platform or in front of the group it is your room. You have, in fact, been given a great opportunity. You can take command, be in control. Everything that happens in the next half hour or whatever time you have is down to you. Get this wrong and you can't really blame anybody else – this is all about you.

So it is vitally important that you feel confident and comfortable about this space that is going to be yours – even if it is only for a short time. So like everything else in the presentation game we need to check it out. And when we've checked it out what do we do? We check it again (see box).

First, find out exactly where the room is located. I worked with a pharmaceutical company once that changed the venue for their annual conference. Organizers were so busy telling all of the attendees about the new site that they forgot to tell the keynote speaker. He showed up at the old venue to discover there was no conference. He should have checked again that nothing had changed – so should you.

I moderated a conference where the main speaker (a local politician) never arrived. Turns out that the speaker went to the hotel reception to ask where to go for the meeting, was misdirected to the wrong conference room, and actually made the speech to the wrong group of people! The story was so amusing that it made the local paper. Find out the exact location, then double check right before the event.

Never Take it for Granted

The other day a friend of mine was on a training program with two other people. They arrived early, checked out the room and the equipment. They made a few changes; made sure everything worked and went outside to join the course participants for coffee. When they came back 15 minutes later, there was no sound and no vision. Mysteriously, in that brief interlude it had all failed. The purpose of my story is that this is what happens more frequently than anyone realizes. Systems fail. Usually it is down to some human messing up somewhere along the line and turning the wrong switch, but the fact remains this is the reality of the professional presenter. So, before you start, never, ever take anything for granted. Work from that basis and you won't be disappointed. A little paranoia is a healthy thing here.

What we are going to do now is go through the checklist that means your room – because it is your room – works as best possible.

As soon as I get to any meeting, big or small I ask to see the room. Often I come back to a room month after month or year after year. Doesn't matter, I always insist on seeing the room. If the organizer tells you, "Oh the room's fine it's the one you used last year," insist of seeing the room. Why? Rooms change. Think about it. Every meeting room changes. The layout changes, the equipment changes. Rooms get refurbished, re-equipped. You need to know what's in the room and what it can do for you. If you don't know that, you haven't done your job. And, no, don't leave it to someone else to check it – do it yourself! It is your responsibility, because it is your room.

The Sound and the Acoustics

One of the most frustrating – possibly just stupid – things I know is a presenter standing on a stage and saying to the audience, "can you hear me OK?" Whatever are they thinking? Surely they can't be serious, can they? I mean the time to know how the sound works is before you start to speak, not while you on for real. If you want to turn off the audience or get them distracted this is a great way to begin. What I want to see in a presenter is someone who is professional, and that doesn't include asking the audience for advice on whether they understand what I am saying.

The time to check out the sound is long before you get onto the podium. If you can get a full sound check the day before do it. Also if you can sit in the room where the audience will be and listen to others do that too. Every room seems to have some sort of individual quirk of its own. I don't know why they just do. But find out what they are.

Also remember, just because you did a sound check the day before, doesn't mean that someone hasn't messed up. That's why on conferences two of my favourite slots are first speaker and right after the morning coffee break. Why? While the participants are drinking down the brown liquid that passes for coffee, you can do another, last minute sound check and make sure the microphones are fully operational.

Also familiarize yourself with the acoustics. Are there echoes or flat spots? If there are try and make sure you stand where they are least likely to affect your delivery. The audience is there to hear you, not your echo. This usually isn't too much of a problem if you are standing in a fixed spot on the platform, but if you have the habit of moving around then it can lead to parts of the audience missing out on some of your speech.

More About the Sound

Today's technology is wonderful, but for some reason sound systems – rather like ventilation systems – seem to be stuck in the Stone Age. So much so, that it really is important that you get the sound checked out as much as possible before you begin. There's no point in creating that great presentation only to discover that the venue's sound system has let you down and the audience is struggling to decipher your speech. Also sound systems vary widely not just in quality but in the type available. Make sure you know what's on offer at the venue. For example if mobile microphones (the type that clip to your jacket or shirt) aren't too reliable, just use a standing microphone or the one on the lectern. Remember the objective of the exercise is to be heard.

Susan Says

Try to arrive early so the technicians can do a good sound check and set the system level for your voice.

The comedian Bob Hope was an amazing performer and he always insisted on rehearsing – on site – and so did anyone who was working with him. He always had a couple of extra microphones (all with brand new batteries) ready to go in case the one he was using stopped working.

Find out where to turn off piped "elevator" music as well. I was making a speech in London once when suddenly a rousing rendition of God Save the Queen started blaring over the speakers.

Switch Off That Mike

Microphones don't just cause trouble because they don't work, they also cause trouble because they work too well. Some years ago I was at a conference where the speaker after lunch was "miked up" by the technician a few minutes before the start of his session. He was "live" on stage. At the last second – realizing he had a few moments to spare – he decided to pay a visit to the men's room. Only problem, he still had his microphone on. Well, at least the audience clapped when he came back, a novel, unique way of opening a presentation you might say! Even, those you would imagine would know better, like Prince Charles, Tony Blair and George Bush have been caught making statements they thought were private in front of live microphones!

Where possible – and assuming the room is not too large – I feel very comfortable not using any microphones at all. Obviously you need to be the judge of this yourself, keeping in mind that the overall objective is to be heard by everyone, not just those in the front row. Indeed, in smaller events a speaker with a microphone creates an unnatural barrier and often they are too loud. It's your call (don't push your voice over its natural threshold), but make sure this item is on your checklist to decide on when you get to the meeting venue.

Climate Control

Virtually every conference room in the world has just two temperatures – too hot and too cold. Too cold and the luckless participants fidget around, putting on jackets and pullovers and not listening to much of what you are saying. Too hot and they are fanning their faces with your presentation notes! Really, really hot and they just doze off.

Of course, the climate is controlled by the technicians, most of whom I suspect of growing tomatoes and other hot-house vegetables under heat lamps in the no-go areas of the basement. But it is still worth asking them if they can turn things down a degree or two, just enough to make sure you get people's attention when you most need it.

If you have a choice of the room being slightly too warm or slightly too cool, go for the second option. Space heats up when the audience arrives.

The Podium and Lectern

A podium is what you stand *on* and a lectern is what you speak *from*. Personally, I try and get as far away from podiums and lecterns as possible. I think a lectern is an unnatural barrier between the speaker and the audience (remember my earlier story about the Geneva Press Club?) But I also recognize that for the less confident it provides the equivalent of a security blanket. Or as someone once said, "something to grip onto with your white knuckled hands."

Also lecterns are useful if you have a lot of notes, especially if you are involved in a complex, or highly technical explanation. But, where possible, try to come out from behind the defensive shield of the lectern and engage with the audience up front. It may horrify you at the outset, but the audience will appreciate it and you'll come across as a lot more natural, friendly and approachable. I often use the lectern so that it is on my left and not in front of me. That way I have access to my notes but the lectern is not as much of a barrier as it would be directly between me and the audience.

Today's lecterns come in all shapes and sizes from the very hi-tech to no-tech at all. Make sure you know what features are available to you. Can you press buttons to change visuals, change lighting and so on? I still prefer using my own remote mouse to control as much as possible.

Podiums come in all shapes and sizes too, although many of us forget that. There is nothing more embarrassing for the more vertically challenged than finding themselves following a really tall presenter, only to realize that the podium is set so low (or the lectern and microphones are set so high) you can't see over the lectern! Does it happen? Oh yes, more than you would think. Even Britain's Queen Elizabeth – who you would have thought knew better – was caught out. She followed President George Bush (Sr) who was significantly taller than she, on stage, so the microphones were set far too high for her. The resulting picture of her fancy hat and not much else above the microphones made the front pages of newspapers around the globe. Someone on her staff probably had a few "guest" nights in the Tower of London for that faux pas!

Of course, everything Queen Elizabeth does is noteworthy. There were headlines all over the world about the so-called "Talking Hat" incident, so, the following day in front of the US Congress, (with all microphones properly placed and she in complete view) she waited for her introductory applause to die down and then she said, simply, "Can you see me?" A discreet acknowledgement to the slip up from the day before, and the whole episode was forgotten.

Here again the lesson is clear. Check out the equipment (or if you're lucky, train someone on your staff to do this, but still make your own final check) and see that it is set up for you, not the previous or following speaker. A very tall and self-important CEO I know always has the technicians set up the lectern for him (he doesn't need a podium), no matter what time of day he is speaking. This usually results in a series of lesser speakers struggling to be seen by the audience during the earlier part of the day. Possibly another good reason for not relying on lecterns and podiums.

The Lighting

You may think that Mr Average Joe presenter has little need to worry about lighting. While that's true for small seminars and workshops, bigger events demand lighting (and lighting technicians) so it is useful to know what to expect. As with everything else, most of what goes wrong on a platform is caused by not being prepared.

If you do end up speaking in a large auditorium you will inevitably have lighting to contend with. And I use the word "contend" deliberately. Because for those not used to having it around it can be very disconcerting indeed.

Let me explain. You've prepared your speech, rehearsed it, tested the sound and checked out the room. Then comes the big day and the big moment and "*surprise!*", there's a great big spotlight shining right in your face! Not only can't you read your notes, you can't even see the edge of the platform, much less the audience. All those reminders about making eye contact are a waste of time. All you are doing is blundering about, except you are doing it in the light not the dark!

And that's you in the dark. Yes – just you. The audience can see you, they can hear you. Great shame, that you can't see them! Somehow all that stuff you've been told about coming out from behind the lectern and making eye contact just doesn't happen.

Here we go back again to the central theme – check it out, every time. Ask, ask, ask!

When they do a sound check, make sure they put on the lights, the way they will do tomorrow, when you are on stage and the audience is there. If it blinds you tell them. The time to say that is before the action starts; before the audience is in their seats; before you want to tell them your story.

For most once-a-year type presenters lighting is a whole new experience. In honesty, its scary, frightening, not something we're at all used to. It reminds us of all those movies we seen about interrogations. Why? It is invasive, it disorientates us – especially when we don't know it is about to happen.

Like everything else, lighting needs to be controlled – fully. Make sure those technicians explain. Make sure you can tell them what you want. Remember it's *your* show – not theirs.

That great marketing guru and Harvard professor, Ted Levitt always got the lighting crew down from their little control box as soon as he arrived at a venue. He knew how lighting worked and what it could, or could not, do for him. He also knew that by engaging these guys in conversation – becoming part of the mysterious brotherhood of technicians – that he could ask, and get, what he wanted. He understood that it was his show, just as much as you need to realize that it is your show. Yes, don't forget it is all about you. These technicians can make or break your presentation. Get to know them and let them know what you want. Oh, and be nice to them too.

Susan says
You can go for years without ever having to worry about lighting, but when it happens it's most likely a big occasion. Keep that in mind and be ready.

So, make sure those lights won't blind you. Make sure you can see the edge of the stage or platform (yes, people have been known to miss that edge and fall into the orchestra pit). Make sure you can see the audience. If you can't it's your room, it's your show, get them to change it. If they don't like it, make them change it anyway. You have one shot on this platform, those bored technicians do it every day. Which is why they don't want to bother to change the status quo. But if you ask them in the right way, they'll be pleased. Bust them out of their boredom, they may even thank you for it!

Making Eye Contact

Assuming that you can get the lighting issue fixed, the other thing you need to consider, especially up on a stage is making eye contact with the audience. It stands to reason that the bigger the room, the more distant you are from the object of your message. This is especially true where there is a raised stage or platform. While I am not advocating that you jump into the audience like some Las Vegas crooner, it does create a much more intimate ambiance if you look down and make eye contact with people in the first few rows. The simple act of doing this makes you appear a lot more approachable and friendly, just like getting out from behind the protection of your lectern. Some of us may not find this a particularly easy thing to do, but it is worthwhile making the effort. Like Charles Aznavour with the crowd of 1,000, he couldn't really SEE all of those people, but he had checked out where they would be sitting and then lifted his eyes to every part of the room, going beyond the blinding spotlight to make everyone feel he looked at them directly.

The Visuals

Susan says

Whenever possible, position the screen(s) for the slides on the side(s) of the stage and the lectern, or your speaking position, in the centre. This reinforces the concept that you are the message and the slides are there to support you.

I know we have "looked" at the subject of visuals in Chapter Six, but there are a couple of points that need to be made here too. Most important of all is making sure that the audience can see them properly. My advice to anyone working in a big room or auditorium is to go and sit in the very back row and get someone to run through your visuals for you. Can you see them OK? Many of us work most of the time in small rooms and it is all too easy to forget – or just not know – that what looks good on a screen in a room of 25 people just isn't the same with 250.

Not only that, check out how readable some of your visuals really are. This is especially important if you have to give technical presentations that involve complex diagrams. As with everything else, your job is to reach the audience with your message. Poor choice of visuals means that part of that message doesn't reach its target. And we have to consider the lighting issue again, even if it is just a little too much sunlight right in the middle of your PowerPoint slides.

The Technical Crew

I always make the effort to get to know the technicians and encourage them to do the things that I want. Technicians are no different from many other workers. They have their little routines and they don't always like change. Most of them have never made a presentation, so that routine is based on what the last guy wanted. So if you are planning to get the most out of them, it pays to be nice – at first.

But it is your show, your moment in the limelight. You own the stage and it is important that they know that. Most people don't get what they would like to have because they just don't ask. Don't be shy. Be polite, but firm. If you want a light in a certain place, ask for it. In 99 percent of the cases you'll get what you ask for. For the other times, throw a fit! That usually works – well it does for me anyway!

Obviously the less complicated your presentation the easier it is for the technical crew to help you. It is interesting to note that most really great speakers – the people who do it for a living day in day out – usually have very little in the way of technical needs. They may have some PowerPoint slides to emphasize a point, but that's all. Everything else is in their head. Amazingly, it always comes across fresher and less rehearsed that way.

Finally, remember the phrase ask, ask, ask? Well again it is better to find out *before* you get to a presentation if you are at all concerned about your ability to use your technology. I was recently part of a presentation where one of the speakers appeared in the meeting room toting a Macintosh laptop. Despite the efforts of the organizer's technical crew they couldn't get his laptop to link up. Result, one very frustrated presenter. If he'd called ahead it could have been very different. Another lesson here is always be prepared for Plan B – go without the slides if need be.

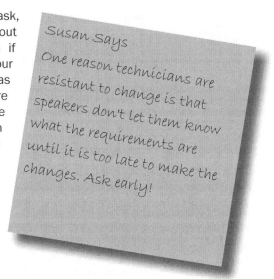

Susan Says

One reason technicians are resistant to change is that speakers don't let them know what the requirements are until it is too late to make the changes. Ask early!

It is, of course, at these times that you realize why many of speakers don't love technicians. Faced with the choice of running out and getting a cable to solve the problem or shrugging their shoulders in that universal, international gesture of hopelessness, the shrug seems to win! Don't say I didn't warn you.

Where do I Put My Stuff?

If there's a lectern on the stage then usually you're OK, because everything you need for your presentation, papers, notes, props and so forth will usually fit into the well inside. If it is a bare stage or platform do the simple thing and ask for a chair or even a chair and table. While this may seem obvious, it can often be overlooked especially if you are nervous about your role. Also many people like to take off jackets at some point in their presentation and you need somewhere to place these. Sounds trivial, but in the heat of the moment it is all too easy to forget the little things. Personally, I like a small table to my left where I can put notes, props, water and so forth. It's easily moved and doesn't get in my way. And it is these little things that often contribute to a great presentation rather than just a so-so one.

Once again, I'll remind you that it is your show so ask for what you need.

What Else do I Need?

Many have a tendency to dry up on the platform. While there are techniques and products to stop this happening (see Chapter Eight), it is always useful to have a glass of water close at hand. Again make sure it's there before you start. If your hand is shaking, don't pick up the water!. You can drink from your glass when the jitters stop. Many times getting onto a platform on my chosen slot (first, or after morning coffee break) I have realized that the technical people have forgotten to replace the water from the previous speaker. Again, small thing that can have big consequences.

The After Dinner Speech Nightmare

I often make after lunch or after dinner presentations. At these, I always make a point of speaking to the kitchen and serving staff to let them know that they should not remove plates (what a loud racket), or serve coffee when I am speaking. It is very disruptive to have that distraction. So coffee containers and desserts are on the table before I am introduced, and no dishes are removed until the event is finished. Servers have told me they appreciate these instructions since they are never sure what they should do when people are speaking after a meal.

Test it, Test it, and Test it Again!

Finally, let me reinforce a key point – never be complacent. Those of us who are born pessimists make the best presenters, because we are always expecting – and consequently guarding against and ready for – the worst case scenario.

Things do go wrong. Hardware, software and people can let you down when you least expect it. So expect it. Anyone who has to make presentations as a regular part of their work gets used to taking precautions and it just becomes a natural process of check, check and check again. For others, who may do it once a year it is much easier to get into trouble.

What I can say is that none of us – no matter how experienced we get – can ever free ourselves of the need to take precautions, take nothing for granted and expect that something will happen when you least expect it. Surely there isn't a presenter anywhere in the world who hasn't got a whole series of war stories to bore fellow travellers with?

Promises, Promises!

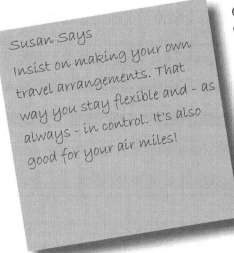

Susan Says

Insist on making your own travel arrangements. That way you stay flexible and – as always – in control. It's also good for your air miles!

Conference organizers, no matter if they are part of your organization or some external firm have one objective – to get a conference (a successful conference) delivered to an audience. In their enthusiasm for doing this, they can sometimes be a little, shall we say, economical with the truth.

They want you to be there because you will enhance their line up. So watch out for conference-organizer-speak. Learn to recognize when the lily is being gilded a great deal.

Even before you get to that room you are going to work in, there are some points that you need to ponder.

Here's a few to get you started:

● "The venue is very close to the airport."

This can be anything from a six to a sixty minute cab ride. It can be worse than that. If you've never been to a venue, ask someone who has. A ten-minute cab ride at a weekend at two in the morning isn't the same as rush hour Monday – been to Kuala Lumpur, Istanbul, Shanghai recently?

● "Tell us when you want to travel and we'll make all the arrangements and you can pick your ticket up at the airport."

Oh no I won't! Because I don't want to spend another hour at some airport desk queuing up to get it." You need to be in control, you need flexibility, don't give that away.

● "The conference hotel is very full, so we are going to put you in another hotel in town."

No you're not. One reason you are going to make that presentation is so that you can mingle with the participants before and after your session. Also if you have ever tried to get to one hotel from another in peak periods, it just adds to the hassle. Try and walk and you arrived wet and windblown, or hot and sweaty. Take a cab and sit in traffic and get more and more nervous.

Am I being extreme in this? Not at all. Organizers have their job to do, you have yours. Yours is to take care of your business and deliver that presentation in the very best way you can. Don't let others get in the way of that.

And that reminds me of what we discussed earlier, before you ever get onto that platform or into that meeting room to rehearse, rehearse, rehearse. You'll thank me for telling you that – wait and see.

Chapter 10

Bad News, Tough Questions and Crises

"The worse the news, the more effort should go into communicating it."

Andy Grove, former Chairman, Intel Corporation

Movies and TV dramas love that line, "I hate to be the one to break the news to you, but...." Well, there's going to be a time when you are quite possibly going to have to do just that – tell unpalatable or potentially explosive news to the world. Anyone in business knows only too well that we don't always have a smooth ride, there are usually some rough edges and bumps and scrapes along the way. Sales crash, business takes a dive and someone has to get up and tell the troops what's going on. Well, while I can't say that most people relish this role, the professional communicator needs to be able to handle it. And the more professional the better it is for everyone.

In this chapter, I want to explain three things:

- how to deal with and deliver bad news
- how to handle tough questions
- how to stay cool when it all goes horribly wrong

How to Deal With and Deliver Bad News

Someone once said that "bad news is just good news that people don't want to hear." Can't argue with that. But if we want to be well-rounded, capable-of-anything speakers, then we need to be able to take the rough times with the smooth times.

And as every cloud has a silver lining, you'll find that taking on difficult tasks like communicating bad news makes you a very valuable asset to any organization. Whether, of course, you want to be noted for that ability, is another question entirely.

Is honesty really the best policy?

Yes, honesty is the best policy, there's just no doubt about that. What many companies never seem to grasp these days is that we are part of a knowledge society. What that means is that most of our colleagues are smart. Years ago, I am sure that organizations could pull the wool over the worker's eyes (certainly some tried to), but you can't get away with that sort of behaviour today. Telling it like it is, playing it straight are the expected norm. If you try and hide the real truth, chances are it will come out very quickly. Employees today have many sources of information and easy access to them. Try and hide and you will be found out and just make matters worse.

Sure the truth may be unpleasant, but it does have the effect of drawing a line in the sand. Once the truth is there on the table, everyone can deal with it in their own way. The truth stops people making up stories about situations. As a colleague once explained to me, "why do smart, sane people believe rumours? Because they are so much more interesting than the truth!"

All too often in a crisis, management forgets to communicate with the internal staff (they are too busy dealing with shareholders and media). In the absence of information, you can always expect *mis*information. And the implications of doing this are enormous – an unhappy workforce can devalue your company very quickly – even sabotage your plans.

Susan says
Need I mention that long term, ongoing communication within your organization will make your message more credible when the tough times arrive? Don't wait for disaster to communicate internally and externally, get a reputation for doing it as the "way we do business around here".

And that is the truth. You can explain, you can predict what happens next, but don't insult your audience. Be honest. They may not like it, but they will respect you for it. Well, most of them will.

Keep in mind that whatever you say may come back to haunt you. Recording devices are everywhere. So be honest and be smart with your comments. Ask yourself if what you are saying today were repeated in six months or a year, would you be embarrassed. Many speakers at the most recent Davos World Economic Forum were trying to explain why their economic predictions from the year before were so inaccurate. Give yourself some wiggle room to account for unexpected scenarios ahead.

Can I be economical with the truth?

The only case for not telling the whole story is where it can really damage the business, or has legal implications that you cannot reveal. You can see this a lot in merger and acquisition scenarios, where the parties are sworn to secrecy to prevent insider trading.

That apart, holding out on bits of the story can only make the overall situation worse. The truth does come out. And as I said before, if you don't tell the truth you create a vacuum. In this case, nature doesn't just abhor a vacuum it fills it to overflowing with rumours and wild guesses of what's really going on. You can, however, focus more on the solution than the problem and still be honest.

The rules for communicating bad news are straightforward. Think right away of the kiss approach (keep it short and simple). Essentially, telling bad news is no different from any other presentation, it requires the same thought processes to make it work. Obviously every situation is different, but the basics don't change all that much.

Plan It

While I'm the first to admit that we don't usually have much time to plan for delivering bad news, that's no excuse not to do it. So start by going back to the SOCO (single overriding communication objective). Ask yourself this:

- What do I want the audience to take away from this presentation?
- What do I want them to *do*?

Now there are lots of ways you can wrap up bad news, but which one do you want to achieve?

For example, do you want the audience to feel, depressed, unwanted, scared or resentful? Most probably not.

Do you want the audience to leave with hope, their pride intact and with a feeling that you're doing all you can to help them? Do you want them to feel empowered to help you deal with this crisis and improve the situation? Most probably yes.

So it is not only what you say that counts, but how you say it. Where you put the emphasis, how you phrase the presentation. Remember, we are being honest here, but we are not creating a collective cry-fest either.

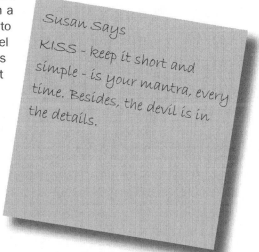

Susan Says

KISS - keep it short and simple - is your mantra, every time. Besides, the devil is in the details.

Therefore, first get all the facts, then quickly write down the key points that you need to emphasize and the core of your presentation. Once you've got that, write it down, get it checked, approved whatever and get on with it. We rarely have lots of time to rehearse these things, and the immediacy has a communication value of its own.

Also short and simple is the way to go. Long speeches contain just too much information. Don't try and get across more than three key points and *never* forget what the SOCO is. Use the SOCO in the opening, in the middle and at the end. For example, let's say you are talking about a downturn in the business; the thing to do is show that the company has a practical plan to deal with this. Emphasize the involvement of everyone in this, and stress that there is a future. That's the one thing you want them to take away – "there is a future at the ABC company, and I'm part of it." I have seen news headlines that read "XYZ company talks its shares lower" because corporate spokespeople dealt with the problems and did not address the solutions.

This means no long speeches, no complex presentations and probably no visuals. Keep it stark and to the point. As one colleague calls it, "get on, get in and get off." Try to balance the good news with the bad news (if you *have* any good news…).

What not to say

Don't plead, don't say sorry and never apologize. Stay professional. If you don't have all of the answers, deliver your message and get off. My view when you have to break bad news is that taking questions at the same time, isn't a good idea. If you can, just tell the story and nothing more. Then schedule another meeting to answer questions when you are better prepared (see below).

Dealing with disaster

This really is a book all to itself, but again the KISS model applies – at least at the outset. Keep it short and simple, tell the facts (check them out first) and nothing else. Never get drawn into speculation or offering your personal opinion. There are many unknowns in a crisis, and for legal and practical reasons, it is better not to hypothesize until you are sure what is happening.

Whether it is some unfortunate event or the breaking of bad news, I've found that working through the checklist below has helped many of my clients prepare themselves for the day that things go wrong. Just by being ready for any eventuality and knowing you are equipped to handle it can help a lot when that day dawns.

How to Handle Tough Questions

Nathan Thomas, former ABC TV correspondent, has interviewed thousands of people from Bagdad to London. He counsels interviewees, "You become the spokesperson. Along with giving factual information, you have the opportunity to put your spin on the issue ...to get your message to the audience. If the interview is confrontational, both you and I will probably know it. Don't lie...don't try to fool me. I do interviews for a living and you probably don't." Good point.

The following are two lists containing all the best advice for handling tough questions that have gleaned over the years. You have two opportunities for dealing with them:

- pre-emptively – before the question arises – in some cases before you even stand up to talk
- in the heat of battle – when you're under fire

In reality you'll need to do both. The only thing to remember is that there is very little you can do after the event so it pays to be ready and to handle them as well as you can when they arise.

Preparing for and pre-empting tough questions

☑ First get the facts, then tell the truth (given your legal parameters). Telling it like it really is doesn't come as an option. Having said that, you need to have planned what you want the audience to take home.

☑ Prepare SOCOs – be proactive not reactive. Positive and professional sum this up. Don't apologize, don't get angry.

☑ Consider recognizing and welcoming visiting experts at beginning. This can be a risky strategy, so be quite clear why you are doing this. You might identify the expert early because you know they will have something to say and it might serve you well to include them on your team.

☑ Be prepared for the worst possible question(s). Because you'll get them! Ill-prepared presenters always attract the most trouble and cause the most as well.

☑ Identify difficult issues and people before the session. You may not have much time to do this, but make as much of it as you possibly can. If you have a crisis plan in place much of this will be self-evident.

☑ Rehearse potential questions and appropriate answers (aloud). Use some trusted people to hear what you're going to say and make them (force them) to criticize you and try and pick holes in your argument.

☑ Identify in advance your team's experts on the topic who may be in the audience. You may want to call on them, depending on whose side they're on.

☑ Use pre-emptive disclosure for issues where you may be vulnerable. Back to telling the truth. Yes, it is better to tell the unpalatable to an audience, before they challenge you.

Answering tough questions

☑ Always make a conscious point of speaking slowly and clearly. You don't want to be misquoted. Also in many cases you'll find yourself being recorded on film or audio. Have printed materials as handouts that summarize your statement.

☑ Listen carefully; don't answer what you thought you heard. If you don't understand it, ask for it to be repeated and repeated again if necessary.

☑ Similarly, repeat questions when you feel the audience did not hear them. You don't want them hearing an answer when they weren't sure of the question.

☑ Pause briefly before answering. Cynics call this the "considered" or "professorial" approach. I call it good sense. Take your time and think of the answer. Don't just blurt out something, that's the way things get confused and you get misquoted.

☑ KISS – especially for hostile questions. Keep it short and simple – every time.

☑ The more hostile the question, the shorter the answer. Don't try and be a hero and don't try and put one over or shame a questioner.

☑ The devil is in the details. You'd better believe it! Less is most certainly more.

☑ Clarify your role/expertise to avoid unnecessary questions outside your area. This is good advice, don't try and answer questions you don't really know much about.

☑ Learn the PEPS[2] method of answering questions: Point – Example/Evidence – Point Restated – STOP TALKING. Make your point, give an example or evidence to back it up, then close with restating your point. It is a sound bite (20 – 30 seconds). Expand the examples or evidence if time allows.

☑ Rephrase questions to defuse them. For tips on this watch any politician on TV. Similarly, do not repeat hostile/unfavourable phrases of a question when answering it.

☑ Avoid judging questions – "Good question," "As I said..."

☑ Be ready to say "I don't know, but I'll be happy to find out for you."

☑ Avoid hypothetical questions if you do not agree with the premise. "What if?" questions are minefields ready to blow up the unwary. Respond firmly with, "I'm not going to speculate on that."

☑ Use the name of the person (if you can) when responding to an angry questioner. If you don't know the name, look at them and say, "I'm sorry, I didn't catch your name or organization." This puts the spotlight of accountability on them.

☑ Do not allow difficult people to speak for a long time (in a forum). Politely ask them to get to the point or to meet later in the interest of the rest of the audience.

☑ Show you understand the other person's position, even if you do not agree with it. Politely distance yourself by responding, "I share your concern, but not your solution." Then leave it at that.

☑ Use up and open body language, especially when you are under fire. This makes you look honest and gets the sympathy of the audience in many cases.

☑ Always look at your questioner and your audience when responding to a question.

2   The PEPS method is a rendition of something I learned from an ex TV anchor and great media trainer, Fred LaCosse in San Fransisco.

☑ Move closer to the questioner, if you can, when taking questions. This puts the pressure and the spotlight back onto them. (This technique is not for press conferences when you would normally stay at the lectern).

☑ If you find a question that allows you to answer and bridge to your nice (positive) closing, use it to end the Q&A session.

☑ Finally, stay positive – even under fire. Never, ever make the conflict personal. It's not professional and you can't afford to do it. In addition, the result will be an emotional response from you, instead of logical, careful messages to the audience.

When it all Goes Horribly Wrong

No matter how professional you are, how well prepared, how well rehearsed, there's going to come a time when disaster strikes. It can be a power outage that leaves you with no visuals and no sound, or the failure of another speaker to show up (or go on for too long). Worse still it can be finding yourself on the wrong end of a hostile audience.

These "out-of-the-blue" accidents can't be avoided (at least I've never found a way), but you can make them a lot less horrible if – like everything else in public speaking – you are ready for even when disaster strikes.

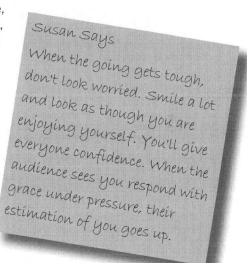

Susan Says

When the going gets tough, don't look worried. Smile a lot and look as though you are enjoying yourself. You'll give everyone confidence. When the audience sees you respond with grace under pressure, their estimation of you goes up.

Wiggle room, or where's plan B?

Professionals call the ability to make do and get through when things go wrong "wiggle room" or, as the British call it, "wriggle" room. Just what can you do to turn trouble into an opportunity? Most often, if you are well prepared you can save the day – and won't the organizers just love you for that.

A speaker's plane is delayed, someone falls ill. If you have the ability to step in and do an extra session, you've helped out and done a lot for yourself into the bargain.

Always have that plan B in your back pocket. All the great presenters can run an extra session, chair a discussion or run a workshop without missing beat. If you can do that you'll open up lots of opportunities, because people will want to work with you. You are a safe pair of hands that they can rely on when the going gets tough.

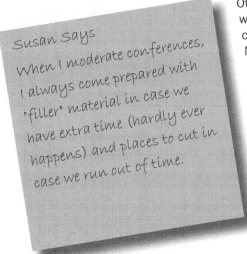

Susan Says

When I moderate conferences, I always come prepared with "filler" material in case we have extra time (hardly ever happens) and places to cut in case we run out of time.

Other needs for wiggle room present themselves when a speaker goes on too long and you have to cut your presentation or when a speaker ends early. Make sure you can mentally cut your presentation quickly (remember, never cut your closing!) , so it doesn't look like it to the audience. Similarly, have some extra pieces you can throw in at a moment's notice. Once again, if you know your stuff, this won't be a problem. Of course, let's not forget that I have spent the major part of this book urging you to not just say "yes" to every request. What I am saying here is, if you can do it – great. But if you are at all concerned about pulling this off – forget it. The one focus has to be on you.

Never blame the hosts

No matter how bad it gets, keep smiling. If the organizers are incompetent or didn't have any back-up equipment, don't complain (at least not until you are back home!). The best thing for you and your reputation is to smile and get on with the job. When the power went out (as I explained above) my colleague just smiled and just got on with things. Everyone wins. You look like the true professional you are, the audience gets what it came for and the organizers are pleased too.

But the next time you work with the organizer who mixed things up, remember to communicate well in advance and double check that things go right.

Keep your sense of humour

I was presenting to over 1,000 people in Washington DC. There were many dignitaries there that day, including Ronald Reagan. I was supposed to enter from the audience, climb the steps to the stage and speak at a stand microphone. As I approached the stage I realized that someone had removed the steps and I was going to have to find a way to get myself on that stage without them. I'm sure I made what was the most ungraceful entry onto a platform in history. I remember thinking that if I were lucky, the floor would just swallow me up and I would disappear completely. Nevertheless I managed the jump and kept (to some extent) my sense of humour and dignity. The presentation went very well. I decided that if I could survive that ghastly entrance, I could survive anything else.

When Rudyard Kipling wrote the first lines of his famous poem "If", he could have been thinking of the professional speaker:

If you can keep your head when all about you
are losing theirs and blaming it on you...

.... Because that is what the effective speaker, the real communicator, is able to do. Trouble comes, disaster strikes, a day's program is in ruins, but you can just get on with it. You know what to do. And the trick here is always keep your sense of humour. Look at the positive, be proactive. As the Nike slogan says, "just do it."

Make that work in the midst of adversity and you know who the audience will remember when it's all over? You!

Chapter 11

When the Boss Cries "HELP!"

"The right to be heard does not automatically include the right to be taken seriously."

Hubert Humphrey, Vice-President of the U.S.

While in the process of putting this book together I saw the chief executive of a major corporation (they are in the coffee business and that's all I'll say) commit professional suicide. Why? The audience went to sleep. They were the victims, he was the perpetrator. Somewhere a corporate scriptwriter or public relations advisor should have been reassigned to outer Mongolia and never allowed near a keyboard again. The reason the audience went to sleep was because the guy was boring in the extreme and showed no personal commitment to the message. All he talked about was his boring mega-corporation and how much he loved it, at the same time injecting not one ounce of originality, excitement or personality. Was it his fault? Well, sort of, because he should have been bright enough to see it was rubbish. But the person really responsible was whoever put it all together.

From the first few minutes you could see the speechwriting work of someone who didn't want to offend anyone, not the client (the boss) not the company lawyers, not the conference organizers and certainly not the audience. In the process they achieved ultimate plain vanilla blandness that is almost impossible to comprehend. Even the front row, usually full of keen, eager nerds was dozing in a post lunch stupor.

For me, as a professional speaker, it was an eye-opener. It was great. It was a textbook version of what you must never do. This chief executive turned off 200 people single-handedly. The reason for it was that whoever prepared his material had no idea how to deal with the boss when the scary cry of "it's speech time" echoed through the corridors of power.

Every so often, in just about every business, the boss gets asked to make a speech. Usually it is something he or she can't say "no" to ("They've just invited us to speak at Davos!"), and so they reluctantly accept. It might be their boss, their best customer, their staff, or a very hot prospect – doesn't matter. They are going to have to deliver this.

Trouble is they don't have the time to do it. So they turn to you. And, as with everything else in life, this moment is what you make of it.

The Best or the Worst Moment

When the boss, or anyone higher in the corporate pecking order asks you for help it is going to be one of two things:

- the worst experience of your working life
- the very best experience of your working life

You have to decide which it is going to be. And, "yes" the decision to go for the brass ring is mostly in your hands.

Welcome to the Circus

Taking on an assignment like this means that you have effectively become the leading act in your own corporate circus. In this circus you get to be a whole series of players. You are:

- the ringmaster: yes, you get to crack the whip
- the lion tamer: with the CEO and top management as the lions
- the clown: you'd better make it fun!

You Need a Plan

Susan Says
One thing you must insist on is a meeting with the person you are writing the speech for immediately. Five minutes will do, but this is critical to success. Before that meeting, get the context for the presentation, the agenda, speakers' list, audience and issues.

What you need to do when the call comes is make sure that you are going to create the best presentation your boss has ever seen. Creating it is the easy part. Getting him or her to deliver it the way it was intended is a whole other game, (one reason I started coaching speakers was so I could recognize the material I was writing). So the first thing you need is a plan. The plan needs to cover content and style, but most of all it needs to have some deadlines.

Let's say that this big speech that your boss has entrusted you to create is due in six weeks time. What are going to be your deadlines?

What you need are deadlines that cover:

- the outline
- the speech draft
- the visuals
- the rehearsals
- the pre-speech briefing

First thing to realize is – unless you work for some exceptional individual – you will be working under one major handicap – no co-operation. You see this speech (that has suddenly become an important part of your life) isn't registering on anyone else's radar screen or Richter scale. You are on your own. How well you survive this test may have a deep impact on your future.

The outline

Unless you know your boss – or whoever it is you are doing this for – intimately, never go away and try and develop a script from the start. First things first, means scoping out a rough draft that has all the points you need to hit. And that should only come after one other critical point has been achieved – a briefing with the boss.

Insist on this briefing – no matter how busy he or she is. Reason? There are so many times I have heard senior executives say, "just write me up something," only to realize that what they get back has nothing to do with what they really wanted to say. Most of the time, senior executives are thinking about four or five things in parallel, so it is all too easy to ask someone else to take this kind of thing off their hands. Problem is they haven't thought it through.

Therefore, insisting on that first meeting to get a "feel" of what the boss wants is critical to the rest of the plan.

It may only last five minutes but it should give you enough basic ammunition to allow you to go off and put that outline together.

Use the AIMS! model to ask the right questions. Find out what your boss's objective for the presentation is. I'm always amazed to find that when I ask someone, "what is your objective here?" they don't know the answer. Helping them to identify the actual outcome they want from the speech is the only way to begin.

Then you move through the model, using Post-its again if you like, to find out what the content should look like. You will see that three logical topics emerge, and the boss should be able to give you some good examples and evidence to fit into the speech (or at least point you in the right direction of where to look).

None of this discussion is time consuming. It should move fast. I have interviewed people in elevators, taxis on the way to the airport, and once I had to continue my initial interview by jumping on the airplane too. I have sometimes brought a tape recorder along to make sure that I use the same phrasing of the words that speakers use in the interview (or just take very accurate notes). It should sound like their words, not yours.

Having all that material to work with means you can now move on to develop your outline.

Now remember, an outline is just that. Possibly only 10 or 20 bullet points that show the beginning, middle and end, emphasizing the key points of the presentation. Where possible have your "client" agree to the approach (this makes things so much simpler later on).

The draft

With the outline agreed, you can now move onto the draft of the speech. How you put this together depends very much on who you are creating this for. Some people just want a set of notes or cards with some key points on them. Others require a full script, with where the visuals go and where to emphasize key words clearly marked.

What you end up doing is very much dependent on who you are writing for and the context of the presentation. By that I mean if this is for a small, informal group in your own office it is much less likely to require a script. On the other hand if it is the annual shareholders meeting or an analysts briefing, you want to make sure that every "I" is dotted and every "T" crossed.

Depending on these circumstances, get the boss to sign off on the draft and you can then work up a final version.

The final script

The word "final" is probably wrong. Indeed I wonder if there is ever such a thing as a final script. Great speakers seem to be forever fiddling with the words and phrases right up to the last minute. Similarly CEOs know that they live in a world of constant change and surprises, so a script (no matter how hard it has been worked on) seldom stays current or useful for long. Because of that, it is important to pay attention to any evolving situations (financial results, emerging regulations) so they can be added to the script as necessary. And you want your boss to make those changes and additions. The end result should reflect what he or she wants to say. If the coffee company CEO I mentioned earlier had helped shape his presentation, the effect would have been entirely different – well at least I'd like to think so!

The visuals

Again, it depends a great deal on the context of the presentation and where it will be given to determine the type of visuals required. If it is a cozy pep talk or a "motivate the troops" type of event then my view is the fewer the better. And best may be none at all. Those type of events cry out for following the KISS rule to the letter. You don't need visuals; you want the speaker's personality to shine through.

However, there are lots of times when you are required to prepare the big production number. What this means is getting some visuals that make sense so the audience sees them, takes in (quickly) the information and gets their attention back to the speaker.

Rehearsals

With the script in the bag and the visuals locked in the PC, the fun is only just beginning. Next comes the part that separates the good presentation creator from the bad and the downright incompetent.

Remember my story at the beginning of the chapter about the CEO who bored the audience to death? Well it's all too easy just to cook up some bland words and leave it at that. Only thing is, if you do that you haven't done your job. Because what you need to do is make sure that your boss (or whoever), the business and by association YOU, give the best presentation you can.

Susan Says

Bland is bad, bad, bad! Think, "what's going to make the audience sit up and take notice?"

You need access

So the first thing you need is courage! Why courage? Because you've got to get access to your "client." CEOs (the heads of anything for that matter) are busy people. Trying to get them to concentrate on an event that could be weeks away is practically impossible, but you have to do it. The reason is that you don't want to turn off that audience; you want to turn it ON. And by asking you to take responsibility for creating the presentation, you have de facto assumed the role of ensuring that success. It doesn't matter than no one else in your organization cares one bit about this – you have that responsibility. Don't forget you are the lion-tamer and ringmaster in all this. For a short period it is you that has the power.

You need rehearsal time

The best way to ensure the success of a presentation is to get your "client" to rehearse. Ha! ha! very funny! Just you try and get the CEO's attention to run through your magical script. Yes, you're supposed to do it. Yes, it will ensure success. Yes, it will make certain that any little problems are ironed out. Does he want to be bothered with it? No!

But this is your responsibility, so you have to find a way. And often the best way is to get to him or her outside the usual business hours. Not only are they likely to be more relaxed (and you can see more of the real person underneath), but they'll have the time to put into it without too many distractions.

What you don't want to hear are the words, "OK, I've got ten minutes between meetings, let's run through it quickly now." Because you just know that those ten minutes will be five and there'll be at least one interruption.

So find your new best friend to help you out and work on getting the CEO's undivided attention.

Your new best friend is your "client's" personal assistant (PA)

The PA knows everything. What you've got to be able to do is to get onto the agenda at times when getting a real rehearsal is feasible. Talking this over with people who have often found themselves in this position, I have come up with some thoughts for you that just may help.

The end of the day isn't very good. Even the most hyperactive executive is running down by this time (because they've been working since 6 a.m.). Also they tend to be a lot more critical and likely to make unnecessary changes.

Early in the morning IS good. Get them fresh and in a good mood

Go travelling with them. Train, planes and automobiles are great places for impromptu rehearsals. Hotel rooms are great for real run-throughs (or book a meeting room in advance)

Go home with them. Yes, this is a good tactic. I'm not suggesting you move in, just carve out a slot on a Saturday morning.

All this, of course, take persistence and courage. But it does pay off.

You need to learn to be critical

Unfortunately, you have to go from being grateful for the time to rehearse to being critical about the performance. Remember my opening remarks in this chapter? Clearly what had happened was that no one felt confident enough to tell the boss that this wasn't the type of thing he should be boring an audience with. So you have to be very objective, very professional and if it isn't working or he doesn't sound like he means it, say so. I think that this is why companies bring me in from the outside – to tell the top management what people on the inside are often afraid to say.

One of my colleagues recounts a story of rehearsing a very senior oil industry figure. He had been working on the script for weeks. Finally, only the day before a major event where his client was to give the keynote speech they got time for a full rehearsal.

Just two problems:

● first, the room was full of the "client's" hangers on (otherwise known as vice-presidents of not-very-much).

● second, the "client" delivered the presentation in a bored, monotone

Amid all this, my friend, stuck up his hand at the back of the room and said: "Next time you do it, can you sound like you mean it?"

There was a shocked silence from the room. But the boss (and perhaps that's why bosses get to be just that), grabbed my colleague and said, "OK, I'll see you in my hotel room at six am and we'll rehearse it until you like it."

They became firm friends. But the real lesson of the story is that courage pays off. Well it does sometimes at least!

154

The stand-in and understudy – this could be your big moment

This is something that few people ever bother to think of, but happens a lot more times than we care to remember. The big speech day comes around and there's a major crisis in the business. Suddenly, this critical speech becomes a lot less important. What happens? Someone else has to deliver it. And this usually comes down to two options:

Susan Says

If the boss backs out at the last minute, don't hesitate. Volunteer. It's your speech isn't it?

- the most senior person who is the least needed in this new crisis

- you

If it were up to me, I'd pick you. And for senior managers who are reading this book, remember there is no point in sending along some senior guy who knows nothing about the speech and will therefore just read it. If you do that, everything that has been worked on goes for nothing. Far better to send you, to deliver a speech you know so well you can dream it backwards – in colour!

Possibly the organizers won't be too pleased – especially if the boss was a key speaker – but that can be more than countered by the actual delivery. This is something not just to think about but have as a contingency plan.

The Pre-Speech Briefing

Scarily, I've given pre-speech briefings while escorting my "client" to the stage to deliver that all important message. You know, the one that's going to change the direction of the business forever. Luckily that doesn't happen every time – but it happens a lot more times than it should.

Again, it is up to you – you're the one responsible remember – to make sure that the boss submits to a pre-presentation discussion. While it may be a last minute run-through, it could also include a mention of key people in the audience, hot issues and tough questions the audience has, late-comers to the schedule, format and so on. Anything you can use that makes the whole effort seem the opposite – effortless.

Assuming that your "client" is able to think on his/her feet a little, the other thing to do is build in a last minute addition that picks up on a topic of the day. This gets the audiences attention and grounds the presentation in "real world issues."

Post-presentation Time

Then, when it's all over try and get some sort of feeling about how it went. Talk to members of the audience, your colleagues, anyone who can give you an honest read-out of what they thought. Did it achieve the objective you had set for it? How was the boss on the platform? What would they want to see instead? What was missing? All these are legitimate and timely questions to ask.

Assessing the impact

Finally, debrief your "client." Make suggestions how to do it better next time. Also, what was their experience like – what would they want to change? Then ask yourself, what did I learn from all this – how can I make it better?

Going Forward

Becoming a person who can be trusted to craft and create winning presentations that hit their mark and delight the audience is a great skill to develop. Better still, it can quickly put you at the heart of the business and close to the people that matter. Most often this is overlooked as a core skill, but it can make a difference to a business. Moreover, it can also make a difference to the way your career – inside or outside the business – develops.

Chapter 12

Finding and Using Outside Help

"Churchill wrote his own speeches. When a leader does that he becomes emotionally invested with his utterances. If Churchill had had a speech writer in 1940, Britain would be speaking German today."

James C. Humes, author of
The Wit and Wisdom of Winston Churchill

Churchill was unique. Most of us can benefit from some outside assistance. Even Barak Obama, another great communicator, collaborates with a professional speechwriter. Sadly perhaps, the heyday of the corporate speechwriter has long gone. In the pre-PowerPoint days, many of the major corporations – the Fortune 100s – had communications staff entirely devoted to creating speeches for their masters. A natural extension of the political and propaganda speechwriters that began in World War II, they have now virtually all disappeared.

Strangely, this has turned out for the worse. Yesterday's on-staff speechwriting professional has been replaced with the amateur communicator with a laptop loaded with software. The PowerPoint Wizard has a lot to answer for!

The problem here is that being a PowerPoint genius doesn't make someone a speechwriter (although it is nice to know one of these). As I have stressed throughout the book, the slides come *after* the message development.

Pre PowerPoint, there was a great deal of professionalism around crafting the corporate message that seems not so visible today. Quality has suffered as the do-it-yourself generation has taken over.

Today if you need help with a presentation you can't just call up the right extension on the internal phone system – those people aren't there anymore. But there are other ways of getting help. This chapter talks about how to find that help and what it can do for you.

Why You Need Outside Help

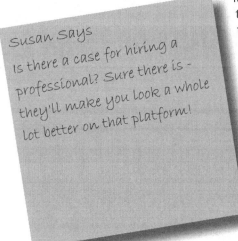

Susan Says
Is there a case for hiring a professional? Sure there is - they'll make you look a whole lot better on that platform!

Most people faced with creating a presentation do it themselves. Tight on time and budget, they seem to think that pecking away on their laptop during their commute or coffee break will suffice. Well for some it possibly will, but if you want to create an impact (and isn't that the purpose of doing it?) seeking out professional help can be both a good idea and make an impact on the bottom line.

Think of it this way. While you're trying to create a presentation you're not doing the job you are being paid for. Neither are you the most objective person on the planet. The idea of getting help is that you do two things:

- bring the outside world into your presentation, anchoring it firmly in day-to-day reality that an audience can relate to

- get professional objectivity. Meaning, if your idea is bad or needs refocus, someone will tell you it is. Because that's why you are paying them.

This can be worth a king's ransom in many cases. You get up on a stage and give a poor presentation and you won't get that critical piece of business. On the other hand, get a professional to help and you will come across just like that – professional. And looking at it from a cost / benefit ratio, the relatively small amount of fees that a professional speechwriter will charge you pale into comparison with the likely business or positive image you can generate.

Where to Find It

Another of my theories of why people don't use professionals to help them craft their presentations these days is that they have no idea where to find them. Unfortunately, this is all too true. Tendency, when pressed is to call up your public relations (PR) firm and ask them. Danger there is that they decide to take the fee and help you. The agency dispatches a twenty-two-year-old account executive who doesn't understand your business. You get frustrated and off goes the self-help cycle all over again. Yes, it's true, have a bad experience like that and anyone thinks it is easier to just fire up PowerPoint and do-it-yourself.

But before you do that. Let's look at some practical options, and why you may want to choose them.

They're staring you in the face

Even before you go outside, look around you. As I made clear in the previous chapter getting someone inside who knows the business can be a great solution. Don't forget to consider this as an option. It can be a great way of testing out someone you think has potential or giving some new experience to a member of your team.

Remember, you are not looking to emulate Shakespeare. If you go down this route what you want is someone who can be logical, understands the business case and hits their deadlines. It also helps if it is someone you get along with and thinks in a similar fashion to you.

The professional firm

OK I was somewhat cynical about the PR firm, but if you have a good one, they'll either have a senior person who can help you or, better still, a list of freelance specialists. Often that's what you'll need – a specialist that understands your industry or the issues you have to tackle in that all important speech.

Many of these people are former technicians who have a gift for writing and creation. Find one of these and you may well have struck gold. These people can bring a whole new view of the industry or the issue, injecting a much needed freshness, energy and excitement into a speech.

> **Susan Says**
>
> Don't commit to an agency or an individual too quickly. Try them out with something small first. Be wary of the consultant who doesn't ask you lots of questions to determine what you want to say.

Similarly, if it is a very complex presentation, having some technical writer look it over and give their opinion can also be a useful way to go.

The fourth estate

Journalists can also be a useful source of speechwriting talent. From generalists who can smarten up and tighten up a delivery with a few well chosen phrases, to specialist writers. These people know their business well. This is particularly true of trade and technical journalists, who not only know your business, but also what your competition is up to. Sign one of these people up and you get a free briefing on your rival's business plan too!

Actors and artists

I've noticed a move recently to get actors and artists involved in presentations. I'm not sure just how effective this is. But I work very much on the premise that if it works for you and the audience you've got to reach, then give it a try. My only thought on this is that you are probably going to have to commit to many hours of rehearsal to get this kind of production right on the night. And while their techniques might help your delivery, their contribution to the actual message might be minimal.

Speech coaches

If you need more help with the delivery than the content, using a speech coach who can be objective – and brave enough to tell you what you're doing wrong – is another resource. Using a coach closer to an event is more effective, especially if the presentation is pretty much ready to go so that a little tweaking and a lot of practice on the delivery take place. Trying to do a complete rewrite of material during last minute coaching is not always effective, and, in fact, may make you less confident if that session occurs very close to the real presentation.

Another benefit of having the coaching close (but not too close) to the actual event is that you must be prepared early. Your deadline becomes, for example, a week before the conference and not the night before.

Building a Relationship

While you may only require outside assistance for a presentation occasionally, having someone that you trust and you know will deliver on time is a great reassurance. Therefore, my advice is that even if it is only once a year (that big sales conference) try and build a lasting relationship. By doing that, you create a resource that you have confidence in, and who knows you, your business and many of the people in it.

Susan says
Check with your legal counsel that there's a confidentiality agreement you speechwriter can sign.

As I have said earlier, having someone like this available just makes things easier and allows you – and most probably your colleagues too – to get on with whatever they do best – making and selling stuff. Often I have seen these sorts of freelancers working for six or seven people in a firm and becoming a key part of the team. Their knowledge of your business, combined with their outside-your-box experiences provides a powerful catalyst when developing presentations that will wow an audience.

One excellent speechwriter I know, Mike Johnson, is an ex journalist. He works so closely with senior management in many companies that he knows what they want to say before the managers do!

One of the great boons of today's communication's explosion also means that you can work with the best you can get practically anywhere in the world. If you are in London, but the best technical presentation creator is in Los Angeles it just doesn't matter anymore. So be creative and think how you can find, secure and develop a relationship with a writer who will enhance your business.

What to Expect

Professional presentation creators work in a variety of ways. Some are there to build a complete speech from start to finish, others to add polish to something that already exists. Still another group are hired to add a real professional polish coupled to industry knowledge that enhances the CEO's personal views.

Counting the Cost

Whatever route you go down, make sure that you agree the basic terms and conditions from the outset. Usually, any professional speechwriter will charge on a time-spent or project basis.

On a time spent basis, fees are charged on an hourly or daily rate (which has the distinct disadvantage of mission creep as bells and whistles get added to the original briefing). With a project basis, you can agree a basic all-in fee from the outset, possibly leaving room for adjustments if you change the brief or ask for extra work that wasn't initially included.

Confidentiality Agreements

Whichever way suits you, get it all in writing and also make sure that there is some sort of confidentiality agreement in place. Speechwriters and presentation designers will almost certainly learn of, or be briefed on, confidential information to make the best job of your speech. You need to be assured that they won't take that information anywhere else.

How to Brief

I'm always surprised how vague and unfocussed people can be when they are trying to explain what they want from a presentation. People who are normally direct and insightful tend to be all over the place, piling up ideas, suggesting alternatives. What you need to do before the would-be speechwriter arrives is have the basic requirements clear in your head. What do you want to communicate and the main points of the speech – the "hot buttons" you need to hit along the way. Be clear on the audience, event, and other speakers. An agenda is helpful to put your presentation into context.

From that information, your chosen speechwriter can begin to construct the draft. Again, make sure you stay as involved as you can (certainly in the early stages) to make sure the whole project stays on track. Once you develop a working relationship you can probably leave a lot more of the actual presentation construction to your chosen professional helper.

Take Them With You

When it comes to the big day, where possible take your speechwriter or coach with you. This way they can see what you – at the moment of truth – made of their work. This really does help them get a much better idea of your strengths and weaknesses in front of an audience. It can also be the useful beginning of an ongoing relationship.

Is It for You?

If you have hired an agency to design your marketing materials, you can see the benefit of hiring a professional to help market you and your message.

Most of us have to deal with creating and delivering presentations as an add-on to our working day. It's another burden for many, which is why we tend not to pay it the attention it should get. But if you have someone you trust, who can deliver the type of material you need then it is probably a worthwhile cost. I'm also betting that it will also make you a much better prepared presenter.

Chapter 13

It's Not Just About Business

"Friends, Romans, Countrymen, lend me your ears."

William Shakespeare, Julius Caesar

Being professional as a presenter, knowing how to put that beginning, middle and end together confidently so it works, doesn't have to be confined only to your professional life. Once you have mastered the basics, being able to speak in front of a group of people has multiple uses.

All of us, no matter who we are, will be called on at some point to give a speech, formal or informal. It may be business related (a colleague's retirement party); family related (a wedding or funeral); or part of a charity drive or sporting event. Doesn't matter what it is, it is good to know that you can get up and address a crowd, whether it be close family or a roomful of strangers.

A Useful Talent to Have

It may have been acquired as a doing business necessity, but being able to present – and being known for it – is not a bad skill to have in your personal talent toolbox. Usually, people who can get up and speak, seemingly unprepared and un-scripted are trusted. Why? Because they fulfil a role that many are too fearful to tackle. Speaking well is considered a leadership skill. Being a reliable speaker can anchor you as a solid member of your group, association, sports club, family or community.

But, you're not addressing the annual sales conference, the shareholders or the analysts meeting. You're talking to your friends, family or close acquaintances. Certainly, your hard won confidence to get up and speak is useful, but so is understanding that you are not running for promotion, not trying to make you the centre of attention this time.

To help convert and channel that corporate focus into a much more personal situation, here are some catch-all rules and advice.

Keep it Short

Even in a business setting no one likes the speaker who goes on an on forever. When the bar is open and the waiters are waiting, this is even more so. So here we are once again back to KISS. Please, please, please don't try and do the great oration of your life, keep it very short and very simple. We will all thank you for it.

It Isn't About you

As I said earlier, this time it isn't about you. Yes, I know the whole book has been about your speech, your terms, you in control and the audience looking at you. This time it's different. When it comes to private stuff, you are the conduit, the information-giver and that's it. Sure you can tell a joke, make people laugh, but it still isn't about you. Who is it about? Whoever or whatever you are talking about: the late, great Aunt Louise, Ben and Natalie's wedding, Laura and Adam's anniversary, Bub's award winning fish. Doesn't matter, it's about other things than you. And by making sure it is not about you everyone will respect you – so you win anyway.

Getting Personal

The first thing to think about is to thank people. The more of them you mention the better it is. Everyone in the world likes to be mentioned. So make a point of recognizing people and thanking them. Recognition is one of those things that the people being mentioned like and the rest of the audience love to hear. It connects everyone together. And it doesn't matter about why you are there or what the occasion is, recognition, singling people out for special mention is a sure fire winner.

Include Everyone You Can

The danger of getting personal is that you might leave someone out. As we all know, decades long family feuds have been built up on the dubious tales of some sort of oral oversight. So throw in everyone and if you can't remember their names, use generalities (e.g. "everyone in the Cooper family who have been so.....”), that covers any eventuality. You can always have a "prompter" sitting or standing close by who can whisper, "You forgot Uncle George," if need be.

Telling Tales and Anecdotes

You may remember the movie *Four Weddings and A Funeral* where some of the anecdotes during these ceremonial events were touching and funny – and others were just in bad taste.

In these types of non-professional situations, humour does work – use it. But use it sparingly and be kind rather then clever or sarcastic. Whether it's a funeral or a wedding people want to celebrate the new or the old – your role is to help them do that.

I wrote earlier in the book about being a catalyst. This role as a speaker at a private event is just that as well. You are the person that binds everyone together. So being kind, to-the-point and considerate are the way to go. Stories about the person or the group are always appreciated. If you have the time and the opportunity it is always helpful to ask around and find out what anecdotes others have. If you do that, try and remember to thank the person you "stole" it from! I worked with a manager who had been asked by the family of one of his employees to speak at the man's funeral. The problem was this manager and his employee had not gotten along very well. Speaking words of praise was awkward for him. Together we found some very good (and true) stories about the man that helped the manager deliver a sincere, positive eulogy.

Finding stories about the people who are being honoured – at either weddings, retirements or funerals – is important. How many of us have sat through a memorial service for a loved one, only to hear a tribute done by someone who obviously didn't know that person. The words could have been lifted from a generic book on eulogies. So ask! Ask for those stories, you'll get them.

Say it from the Heart

I've spent a lot of time in this book stressing the need to tell the truth. Same goes for these family situations. Except replace the phrase "tell the truth," with "be honest". By that I mean say the things that you feel. These events are not about being professional. Controlled yes, but not professional. Be yourself, but use all those techniques you've learned and feel comfortable with as well. Speak slowly and clearly, focus on the audience, keep that message short. Even here there is a SOCO. Knowing what that single overriding communication objective is and making sure it comes through loud and clear should ensure you don't ramble on for too long.

Let the Audience Leave Feeling Good

No matter what the occasion and however solemn or sad, try and lift the audience. Send them home feeling good about whatever you were all there for and feeling good about themselves too. That's what you've learned to do throughout this book. Remember that a great audience is a happy audience and even in these situations where the focus isn't on you, making them smile or think good thoughts is a great way to go.

Keep in mind

- Keep comments / presentation short
- Tell stories / anecdotes – funny and serious – that catch the mood and make the point
- Recognize / thank key people
- Let the audience leave feeling good about the event and themselves
- Make it special

Speaking in public – whether for personal or professional reasons is all about one thing – people. You are trying to do your best to connect with people. There are many ways and many reasons that this happens, but being one of those people who can act as a catalyst is – in the final analysis – a rewarding thing to be able to do.

Closing

This book has taken you through the process of designing and delivering a presentation that has logic, control and impact – both in terms of what you say and how you say it. It has stressed the importance of balancing your own objectives with the needs and expectations of the audience. Also it has emphasized how important each and every presentation – no matter how seemingly insignificant at first sight – can be for you and your career.

So what's next – how can you continue to progress? Here are some simple suggestions to help you climb the ladder of presentation excellence:

Remember, ask questions about the audience, the event and the venue as soon as you can. You can never know too much about an event	☐
Set your SOCO for each presentation. Make that the very first thing you do	☐
Quickly outline your message using the AIMS! Model. Then put it aside and take time (if you have it) to reflect on what you really want to say	☐
Always prepare your message before you put in the PowerPoint slides	☐
If you do use PowerPoint, keep in mind those guidelines for creating professional visuals	☐
Look for props, stories, anecdotes, humour, or other devices that add value, interest, color and excitement to your message	☐
Complete the presentation well in advance (if you can) so friends and co-workers can offer suggestions and comments	☐
Commit yourself to doing what all great professionals do –Rehearse! Rehearse! Rehearse!	☐
Sit down after each event and identify the few things you would like to improve and the few you want to be sure to do again and again. Because they worked!	☐

None of these are difficult to do. It's all about working smart rather than hard. It's all about being the very best speaker you can be.

And the reward? The satisfaction of standing in front of a group of people who are really listening and appreciating what you have to say. More than that. Hearing the applause, closing your speech file, turning off the projector, walking away, thinking, "I did a good job. I put my message across and they valued their time here today."

Now that's not just a good feeling – that's a *great* feeling.

In ending this book, it seemed appropriate to find out what had happened to the young man I mentioned in the introduction: the one who had been so impressive speaking to the San Francisco Chamber of Commerce's Board of Directors. So I looked him up. No surprise, I suppose. He isn't just speaking to the Board these days – he's on the Board. He has his own business now and is very successful. You see, as I've been saying all along, Substance and Style are a winning combination and always will be.

May I wish you every success wherever and whenever you speak. Just don't forget that little three letter word – it's all about you!

Appendix

Sample Presentations

Using the AIMS! model, here are three different versions of the same presentation given to different audiences – each with different objectives:

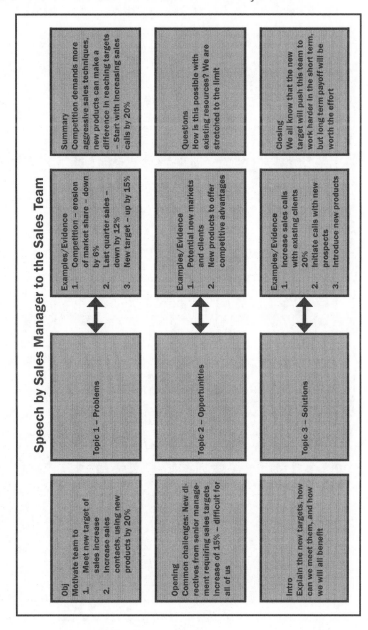

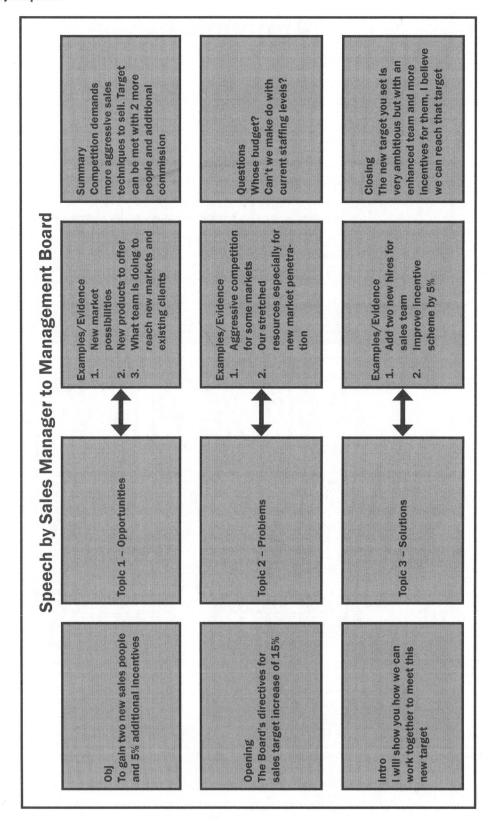

Speech by Sales Manager to Management Board

Obj
To gain two new sales people and 5% additional incentives

Opening
The Board's directives for sales target increase of 15%

Intro
I will show you how we can work together to meet this new target

Topic 1 – Opportunities

Topic 2 – Problems

Topic 3 – Solutions

Examples/Evidence
1. New market possibilities
2. New products to offer
3. What team is doing to reach new markets and existing clients

Examples/Evidence
1. Aggressive competition for some markets
2. Our stretched resources especially for new market penetration

Examples/Evidence
1. Add two new hires for sales team
2. Improve incentive scheme by 5%

Summary
Competition demands more aggressive sales techniques to sell. Target can be met with 2 more people and additional commission

Questions
Whose budget?
Can't we make do with current staffing levels?

Closing
The new target you set is very ambitious but with an enhanced team and more incentives for them, I believe we can reach that target

Speech by Sales Manager to Industry Conference (Peers, Competitors and Potential Clients)

Obj
Make the company look good
so
1. Potential clients will want to meet with us for future business
2. Peers and competitors respect our work

Opening
Common challenges (theme of the conference) on global financial transaction security

Intro
Show how we can win the war on financial transaction vulnerability

Topic 1 – Problems

Topic 2 – Opportunities

Topic 3 – Solutions

Examples/Evidence
Threats to financial transaction security
1. Fraud – % increase
2. E commerce – famous cases

Examples/Evidence
New technology (ours)
1. New products (ours)
2.
3. New cross border co-operation

Examples/Evidence
1. Continued investment in R&D
2. Continued commitment to tailoring products for specific needs

Summary
Demand for security in global financial transactions has never been so high – and individual solutions must be tailored for individual requirements

Questions
Future problems and matching technology

Closing
The bad news is that the danger to transaction security has never been so high. The good news is that our technology continues to be one step ahead of the bad guys

AIMS! Model

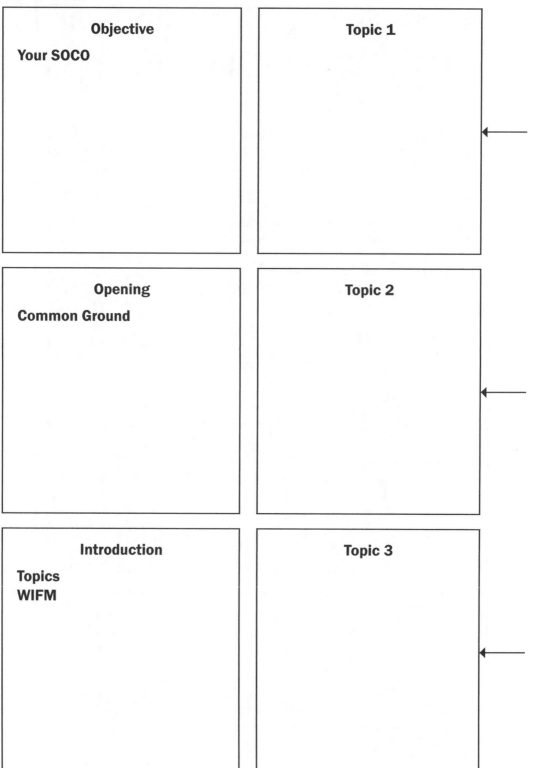

Objective	Topic 1
Your SOCO	

Opening	Topic 2
Common Ground	

Introduction	Topic 3
Topics **WIFM**	

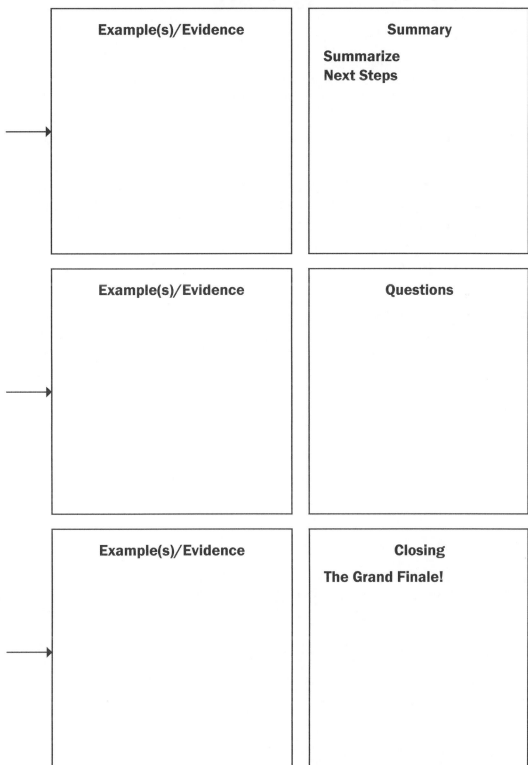

You can download a PDF of this model from www.speechworksintl.com using the password "AIMS".

Example(s)/Evidence

Summary

Summarize
Next Steps

Example(s)/Evidence

Questions

Example(s)/Evidence

Closing

The Grand Finale!

Website

Visit www.speechworksintl.com for more information about Susan and to download copies of the AIMS! Model and sample presentations. Also, you can download special summary cards on:

- Questions to Ask in Advance
- Elements of a Successful Speech
  - The Delivery
  - PowerPoint Tips
- Tips for Handling Tough Questions

To access these downloads you will need to enter the password: AIMS

Susan Huskisson

Susan Huskisson, an American and European-based communication consultant, has more than twenty-five years experience coaching senior executives in presentation skills. She has a broad range of communications experience, from White House Assignments to commercial television and radio.

In addition to teaching others to present, she has spoken to numerous conferences and meetings – with audiences from five to thousands.

She was an instructor at Golden Gate University, San Francisco, has taught at the Graduate Schools of Business, ISA, in Paris, and IMI (now IMD) in Switzerland. She has a B.S. in English Education and an M.B.A. in Management. She is president of Communication Training, Inc.

She works all over the globe, coaching and training SpeechWorks™ Presentation Performance, teaching participants to design and deliver logical, persuasive, and interesting presentations and materials (including better PowerPoint visuals). Attendees learn how to look and sound more professional with any audience, including peers, external groups and senior management

She can be reached at susan@speechworksintl.com

Index